NEW MEDIA
FOR MINISTRY

A Handbook of Strategies and Tactics for Media Ministry Impact

FIRST EDITION

BY BRYAN HUDSON

visionCommunications

INDIANAPOLIS, INDIANA USA

NEW MEDIA
FOR MINISTRY

A Handbook of Strategies and Tactics
for Media Ministry Impact

TABLE OF CONTENTS

INTRODUCTION   7
How to Use this Book
Who Should Have this Book

PART ONE: Understanding New Media

CHAPTER ONE: How Important is Media to the Ministry?   11
What are Media and New Media?
What is the Definition of "Media?"
How is it Different than "New Media?"

CHAPTER TWO: Avoiding The Technology Trap   17
What is Technology?
A Definition of Technology for Ministry:
Technology in the Book of Acts
Technology Misunderstood and Misapplied
Technology is about Method and Process

CHAPTER THREE: Biblical Foundations for New Media   21
Media in the Bible
A Survey of the History of Media

CHAPTER FOUR: What is Web 2.0?   29

PART TWO: Strategic Thinking

CHAPTER FIVE: Strategic & Tactical Uses for Media   35
The Utility of New Media
New Media Strategies and Tactics
Definition of Strategic and Tactical

CHAPTER SIX: The Power of Clear Objectives   39
Why Purposes Don't Prosper

CHAPTER SEVEN: Have you met "ADDIE?"   43
Designing Effective Solutions
Analysis, Design, Development, Implementation, Evaluation

PART THREE: Getting Things Done

CHAPTER EIGHT: Finding Your Productivity Sweet Spot   51
Are You in the Cloud?
Recommended Cloud-Based Productivity Applications

CHAPTER NINE: Getting into the Flow   57
Simple Time Management (Excerpt from *The Power of Less*)
Problems Produced by a Lack of Time management
Time Wasters to Avoid

CHAPTER TEN: How to Hire Help   63
Questions to Ask Before you Hire

CHAPTER ELEVEN: Internet Safety & Security   67
Tactics for Godly Internet Use
Network Security

PART FOUR: Ministering with Media

CHAPTER TWELVE: 21st Century Fishers of Men   73
What Good Fishermen Understand

CHAPTER THIRTEEN: Using Social Media   75
Facebook
Twitter
Create You Own Social Network

CHAPTER FOURTEEN: New Media Toolbox   79
Inside the Toolbox:
Personnel
Promotional Tools
Production Tools
Presentation Tools
New Media Toolbox Assessment

CHAPTER FIFTEEN: What Makes a Good Website?   89
Six Ways to Build a Website
Website Usability Checklist

CHAPTER SIXTEEN: So You Want to Do Video?   97
Video Production Process
Some Types of Video Production
Shooting Better Video with Consumer Cameras
Webcasts & Streaming media
Are You Ready to Go Live?

CLOSING THOUGHTS   105
Recommended Reading
Contact the Author

NEW MEDIA GLOSSARY   107
Submit Suggestions

INTRODUCTION

New Media for Ministry was written to educate, inform and inspire Christian leaders and workers on the practical uses of new media for ministry. This material is presented in an editorial, personal style. Persons who want to gain fresh insight into new media, which represents a convergence of many forms of old and current media, will find many new vistas of understanding. Persons already engaged in various aspects of new media production will be inspired to explore new ways to use their talents and skills in support of the work of God's church and the promotion of the gospel of Jesus Christ.

How to Use this Book

As a handbook, this book is an aid to both ongoing and proposed new media related ministry projects. The Table of Contents contains specific headings that will allow you to go directly to topics of interest.

 The icon shown to the left indicates special content available at the companion website *www.newmediaforministry.com/book*

The website offers ministry aids and Internet links to helpful information and tutorials. The website offers practical, technical and emerging information on the ever-changing world of new media.

New Media for Ministry is not an exhaustive do-it-yourself guide. This is a resource of practical understanding and best practices. As with many other areas in life and work, it is good to know when to engage professionals for demanding projects. This book provides a matrix of concepts and practical considerations that will inform your decisions regarding new media production needs.

Who Should Have this Book

This book is useful for anyone engaged in ministry who also recognizes the increasingly important role of media and new media to ministry. Pastors can use *New Media for Ministry* as a reference for understanding the terms and processes surrounding media. This book also offers many insights on personal productivity and tips on how to make good use of Internet-based tools. Pastors should have a grasp of the concepts surrounding new media so that they can recognize advantages and disadvantages of particular tactics related to media.

Media department staff members and volunteers will appreciate learning about some of the important stages of media production, definitions of new media terms, and tips on project management.

PART ONE: Understanding New Media

CHAPTER ONE
How Important is Media to the Ministry?

W*rite the vision, make it plain on tablets, that he may run who reads it.* (Habakkuk 2:4)

Ministry is all about fulfilling God's purposes in our generation. Pastors and ministry leaders daily grapple with many responsibilities related to obeying God, while effectively leading their organizations. Added to this mix is the question, *"How important is media to the Ministry?"*

The quick answer is, "Very important!"

We live in a media-driven culture. Ours is a culture accustomed to viewing screens and listening to sound bites. There is no avoiding this reality. Said another way, media is *the way of the world in which we live.* The greatest persuasive fact regarding the importance of media is that our most important resource, and the most significant book ever written, the Bible, is a media "product." Moses' tablets, David's Psalms, Habakkuk's written vision, the scroll handed to Jesus on the day He proclaimed His ministry, Paul's letters, your personal Bibles (printed and online), and even the *Book of Life,* are all forms of media.

A better question may be: *"How well is your ministry using media and new media in the 21st Century?"*

In all of human history, there has never been a time when media creation and sharing tools were more accessible than today.

What are Media and New Media?

There was a time when we carried books for reading, loaded compact discs into portable players, listened to music players like Sony's Walkman, visited our local Blockbuster to rent a DVD, took out our laptop computers to send an e-mail, and then stopped everything to answer a call on our cell phone.

That "time" was only as recent as the early part of the 21st century. Today, we can read book content, listen to music, watch videos, send an e-mail and take telephone calls, all on the same device, such as an iPhone or other so-called "smart phone."

This phenomenon is called "convergence." Media content and modalities for both creating and consuming media no longer require separate devices. Not only has the need for multiple devices been reduced, the media itself has been transformed into a digital form that can be downloaded, transferred, and enjoyed on multiple devices. No longer are printed books the only domain for words. Words can be enjoyed and comprehended on devices such as the Amazon Kindle e-book reader. There are e-book reading applications available for all devices from mobile phones, to laptops, to desktop computers.

Every device and technology, including bound books, has its advantages and devotees. Books continue to be a highly efficient and usable "technology." They are inexpensive, lightweight (by in large), do not require any power source, and have no learning curve for proper use. Books also have a permanence that is lacking with digital content. Books cannot be easily forged or changed.

Devices such as the Kindle e-book reader and iPad generate debates about the future need of print media. New media embraces *all forms of media* as elements for communication and interaction solutions among people in their cultural language. Some commentators point to the demise of daily newspapers as evidence of a future without print media.

This assumption only considers the lifestyles of Americans and our other prosperous friends around the world.

As a solution for information dissemination and learning, print media such as textbooks will continue to provide a viable option for literate people throughout our world for many years to come.

New Media has emerged from the convergence of traditional media, technological advances in digital media and Internet communications. New media is an organic, growing field. Like a flowing river, the growth of new media has followed the terrain of our social and technological development. No one person or company, not even Apple Computer, is responsible for the current form of new media.

What is the definition of "Media?" How is it Different than "New Media?"

There is no single standard interpretation of terms in the world of media and new media. These terms are defined by the people, professionals and institutions that use media. Over time a consensus emerges on the use of terms. For example, the term Podcast is attributed to Apple Computer because of its iPod device. In fact, the emergence of podcasts, which began as blog posts that included audio, was pioneered by Windows computer users. Steve Jobs and Apple Computer had nothing to do with the creation and initial growth of podcasting.

Three Common Uses of the Term "Media."

1. Grammatically speaking, media is the plural form of the word *medium*. A medium is an object on which data can be stored. A hard drive is a medium for digital data storage. A cassette tape was a medium for storing recordings using an analog method.

2. Media also refers to various means of communication. For example, newspapers, books, television, radio, and compact discs are different types of media.

3. The term is also used as a collective noun for the press. We speak of "the media" as news reporting agencies.

Originally, the term *new media* was used to distinguish between "old" media such as print or analog television and "new" digital forms of media. Another definition of new media: *"In general, new media refers to new forms of human and media communication that have been transformed by the creative use of technology to fulfill the same basic social need to interact and transact."* [Faiola, Anthony (2001) *New Media Basics: Understanding Message Design Theory in a Post-Information Society.* Hoboken, NJ: John Wiley & Son]

New media is also closely associated with the term, "Web 2.0," which refers to a second generation of Internet-based services, such as web-based applications, social networking websites, blogs, and online collaboration. (More About Web 2.0 in Chapter Four) The "new" of new media refers to the inclusion of the latest technologies, current best practices, and the capability to integrate future innovations.

The term *"new media"* is considered a buzzword among some. Some prefer to use the term *"digital media"* or *"multimedia"* rather than new media. Technically, the term digital media is limited to electronic or binary media that lives on hard drives or other digital storage mediums. Books and flyers could not be classified as digital media, but they could come under the heading of new media when part of a combined solution of media content. New media is a more inclusive concept than digital media.

While traditional or "old" analog media was limited to indelible uses such as print and live broadcast, digital media allows content to be reproduced, re-purposed and revised as needed for various uses. Analog tools such as typewriters could impose text on paper, but the text could not be revised without re-typing. A word processing application such as Microsoft Word converts text to digital bits that may be rearranged, copied, pasted and transferred and finally output to an analog medium such as paper.

More than a specific device like an iPad or a specific software application like Adobe Photoshop, new media is a category that defines a set of tools and techniques that can be used to develop communication and interaction solutions.

New media enables:

1. Emerging new technologies resulting in enhanced human communication

2. Leveraging the Internet and web services (also called "Web 2.0") for purposeful interaction

3. The combining of images, sound, video and text in new ways

4. The development of portable media such as optical discs, digital signs and kiosks

5. Customization in how users experience and interact with content

6. Non-linear access to content. Users can move to any point within digital content, rather than being limited to "turning one page at a time"

7. Synchronous (real time) and asynchronous (time shifted) communication and content sharing

8. Embracing future technologies and innovations yet unknown

9. Project collaboration without regard to time or distance among team members

Current and new forms of media will continue to be a vital part of the work of the church in the future. Again, the "new" of new media embraces all known and yet unknown media and communications innovations.

CHAPTER TWO
Avoiding The Technology Trap

There is a common misconception regarding the meaning of technology. We often view technology as machines, electronics, computers, and gadgets like mobile phones or GPS devices. Discussions about technology usually revolve around innovations by companies such as Sony, Microsoft or Apple.

Interestingly, access to technology (as machines and gadgets) has not always helped people become more efficient and effective in their work. In some ways technology, as it is commonly understood, has caused people to become more distracted, disorganized, and distanced from both purpose and other people.

Without a proper understanding and application of technology, too much confidence may be placed in machines and electronic devices.

What is Technology?

The basic definition of technology comes from the Greek language. The Greek word *technologia* means, a systematic treatment of an art, from *techne* meaning "art," and *logia*, meaning "skill." Standard dictionary definitions of technology include:

1. The practical application of knowledge especially in a

particular area such as engineering

2. A capability given by the practical application of knowledge such as a car's fuel-saving technology

3. A manner of accomplishing a task especially using technical processes, methods, or knowledge such as in designing computer memory

4. The specialized aspects of a particular field of endeavor such as educational technology

A Definition of Technology for Ministry:

Technology is a body of knowledge used to get things done. It is the application of a method to meet an objective or solve a problem. It is the practical, repeatable, application of knowledge and skill in any area.

Example of Technology in the Book of Acts

In Acts 8: 26-40 we read the story about Philip and the Ethiopian official. At first glance, this well-known Bible story is about an encounter between two men, orchestrated by God, that would end with the transformation of an influential Ethiopian.

In this text, we observe **transportation technology** in the form of the Ethiopian's chariot. The chariot was equivalent to the automobiles and roads of today. This transportation technology, as crude as it may seem to us, allowed this high-ranking official to come to Jerusalem to worship. In the plan of God, technology helped this Ethiopian encounter the living Word of God.

This text also shows that as the Ethiopian returned home in his chariot, he was reading the scroll of Isaiah. That scroll represented a form of **recording or information technology**. He was not reading an original scroll from Isaiah's hand. He was reading a copy, or recording, of Isaiah's words on a "device" made of animal skins or plant fibers. This technology conveyed the words of God that moved the Ethiopian's heart towards Christ.

We should also note the supernatural means by which God transported Philip to the location of the Ethiopian as another form of technology. God obviously has His own class of technology!

Technology is more than computers and machines. Technology is about method and process.

Technology begins in the mind. All of us use technology as a *practical, repeatable, application of knowledge and skill.* We create and use tools to help us complete our tasks, but the tools are not the core technology.

Effective Christian leaders install systems and methods for ministry effectiveness. This is an example of technology *without* machines. Too often, pastors and leaders plead technological ignorance and begin looking to tech-type people (i.e. "Geeks") for "deliverance." These pastors or leaders *wrongly believe* that they know nothing about technology.

The old saying is true, *"Do not let the tail wag the dog."* Leaders who may be less technically-inclined, should continue to provide *technological leadership,* from a systems perspective, in churches and organizations. The people who understand the technology of machines often do not understand the greater technology of how God's church operates. There is a divine technology of best practices for the overall ministry, with the Bible and the Holy Spirit providing the basis of it.

Technology Misunderstood and Misapplied

Sometimes, people look longingly towards technology as something that can be purchased that will make the ministry all better. Not true!

Example #1: A person in a church became convinced that the church needed a cash register for the bookstore. In reality, the "bookstore" was only a table in the foyer with some books and recorded media on it. The technology plan for the ministry utilized a computer-based method for tracking purchases using a database computer program. The cash register was not necessary, but to this person it seemed like the missing "technology" that was needed for the bookstore. Since the church would not buy a cash register, the person purchased one anyway. It became little more than an unused prop.

Example #2: A church leader insisted on purchasing a $9,000 HD (High Definition) camera. All the other supporting video equipment was SD (Standard Definition): Analog cabling, a low cost SD video mixer, and small tube televisions for monitors. The capabilities of the HD camera could not be realized using SD equipment. For $9,000, the church could have acquired an *entire* high quality prosumer grade two-camera HD live production solution. The *technology* of High Definition is not a single camera, as impressive as that one camera may be. HD is a technology based on a related set of methods, standards and equipment. Every piece of equipment in the chain must support a HD workflow.

Example #3: A ministry with a small staff is sold an expensive Microsoft Small Business Server solution without fully understanding the technology of computer networks and scale. 95% of the usable functions of a dedicated server can be achieved without owning a dedicated server, at a fraction of the cost.

Again, let's be clear about the meaning of technology: *It is a body of knowledge used to get things done. It is the application of a method to meet an objective or solve a problem. It is the practical, repeatable, application of knowledge and skill in any area.*

Most Pastors and Lead Ministers are Already Technologically Advanced!

Under the above definition, pastors and senior church leaders *should consider themselves technologically advanced!* Their effective methods of sermon preparation, preaching, team building, ministry administration, counseling and more, are all examples of applied technology.

CHAPTER THREE
Biblical Foundations for New Media

The Lord gave the word, and great was the company of those who proclaimed it. (Psalms 68:11)

Does the Bible have anything to say about new media? From the perspective of computers, the Internet and Web 2.0 applications, I would say, "No." From the perspective of meaningful communication, the conveyance of truth, dynamics of human interaction, the influence of positive/ negative messages and promoting standards of godliness and decency, I would offer a resounding "Yes!"

New media is all about the convergence of diverse forms of communication and interaction among people. Whatever engages the hearts and minds of people attracts God's interest. The scriptures address both the blessings and dangers of interpersonal communication.

Concerning the blessing of interpersonal communication, Hebrews reads, *But exhort one another daily, while it is called "Today," lest any of you be hardened through the deceitfulness of sin. For we have become partakers of Christ if we hold the beginning of our confidence steadfast to the end.* (Heb. 3:13-14)

Exhortation and encouragement have a special place among believers in Christ. According to the text, we have the responsibility to communicate with one another in such a way as to help our fellow believers stand against the constant onslaught of temptation and self-deception. It is not inconceivable that we can use Internet enabled new media to fulfill this mandate of exhorting one another. We can also detect dangers lurking among interpersonal communication, *"Do not be misled: Bad company corrupts good character."* (1 Cor. 15:33)

Today, "bad company" is not limited to face-to-face interactions. The influence of relationships can be extended through Internet enabled communications such as streaming media and social networks. There's no end of bad company among the many virtual, but significant, relationships developed over the Internet. I am aware of married couples that "met" and "fell in love" over the Internet. While it is something that I cannot recommend, it is none-the-less becoming a reality in our time.

Media in the Bible

The Bible is the most significant and pervasive media of all time! The Holy Scriptures began as God-inspired words placed on papyrus scrolls and clay tablets by men who wrote as they were "moved by the Spirit." The medium was papyrus, but the word was God-breathed. Over time, holy writings emerged, from the Pentateuch (The first five books, or scrolls, of the Bible), to the scrolls of history (such as the Chronicles), the Psalms, Prophets and all the other scriptures that emerged. These holy writings brought guidance, insight and the communication of God's laws and ways.

When Moses received the Law, God inscribed the words on tablets, a form of media. The prophet Habakkuk wrote, *"Write the vision, make it plain on tablets, that he may run who reads it."* (Hab. 2:4) Clay tablets were the most effective media of his day, both portable and relatively permanent. God did not want His words inscribed on cave walls, but on a form of media that could be shared and transported. It does not require any stretch of reason or imagination to conclude that God would honor the use of modern portable media as we continue to "make the vision plain."

Paul instructed that his writings be read aloud to Christian congregations (Col. 4:15-17). His words that were placed on scrolls became an extension of his apostolic ministry into the churches.

For I indeed, as absent in body but present in spirit, have already judged (as though I were present) him who has so done this deed. In the name of our Lord Jesus Christ, when you are gathered together, along with my spirit, with the power of our Lord Jesus Christ. (1 Cor. 5:3-4)

When Paul stated that he was present "in spirit" among the Corinthian church, we know that he did not appear as an apparition or some kind of metaphysical "apostolic ghost." I believe it is reasonable to conclude that he understood that his words, written on scrolls, carried his heart and passion to the people. It was as if he were present through his writings. Have you ever read a well-written biography and felt as if you were present with the author?

While face-to-face interaction can never be substituted, we should not underestimate the capacity of recorded words to convey something of the substance and presence of God to readers. This was true when the Bible was a collection of scrolls. It is true today, now that we have the completed canon of Holy Scriptures. It is also true when I begin my sermon by reading God's Word from the screen of my iPad.

Modern Bibles, as books, continue to be the most efficient, cost-effective and readily available media for the conveyance of God's Word. But we should also concede that book-based Bibles are not the only media form that God is using to convey His word.

If we can view new media in the light of a God whose presence is pervasive and progressive in the affairs of mankind, then we should seize upon the opportunities that utilizing new media affords to the work of Christ.

Looking toward the end of this age, we read in the Book of Revelation that the eschatological sequence of events is triggered by Christ himself with the breaking of "seals" in opening the "scroll," which is clearly some form of heavenly media.

And no one in heaven or on the earth or under the earth was able to open the scroll, or to look at it. So I wept much, because no one was found worthy to open and read the scroll, or to look at it. But one of the elders said to me, "Do not weep. Behold, the Lion of the tribe of Judah, the Root of David, has prevailed to open the scroll and to loose its seven seals." (Rev. 5:3-5)

Clearly, heaven has its unique form of communication through media. John's descriptions could only be understood by reference to earthly forms with which he was familiar. A scroll in heaven is not the same type of scroll on earth. What we understand is that the concept of using some form of media to communicate an important message is a consistent practice in heaven and on earth.

A Survey of the History of Media

*(**Author's note**: Some dates are approximate. The author's additions to this time line are highlighted and italicized.)*

3500 BC to 2900 BC	The Phoenicians develop an alphabet. The Sumerians develop cuneiform writing - pictographs of accounts written on clay tablets. The Egyptians develop hieroglyphic writing.
1775 BC	Greeks use a phonetic alphabet written from left to right.
1400 BC	Oldest record of writing in China on bones.
1400 BC (est.)	Giving of 10 commandments by Moses on tablets
1270 BC	The first encyclopedia is written in Syria.
900 BC	The very first postal service - for government use in China.
776 BC	First recorded use of homing pigeons used to send message - the winner of the Olympic Games to the Athenians.
500 BC	Completion of original Hebrew manuscripts (39 OT Books)
500 BC to 170 BC	Papyrus rolls and early parchments made of dried reeds - first portable and light writing surfaces.
200 BC	Completion of the Septuagint Greek Manuscripts
200 BC to 100 BC	Human messengers on foot or horseback common in Egypt and China with messenger relay stations built. Sometimes fire messages used from relay station to station instead of humans.
1st Century	Completion of original Greek manuscripts (27 NT books)
14	Romans establish postal services.

37	Heliographs - first recorded use of mirrors to send messages by Roman Emperor Tiberius.
100	First bound books
105 BC	Tsai Lun of China invents paper as we know it.
305	First wooden printing presses invented in China - symbols carved on a wooden block.
1049	First movable type invented - clay - invented in China by Pi Sheng.
1384	Wycliffe produces hand-written manuscript copy of the complete Bible
1450	Newspapers appear in Europe.
1455	Johannes Gutenberg invents a printing press with metal movable type.
1526	William Tyndale's New Testament; The First New Testament printed in the English Language.
1560	Camera Obscura invented - primitive image making.
1611	The King James Bible
1650	First daily newspaper - Leipzig.
1714	Englishmen, Henry Mill receives the first patent for a typewriter.
1793	Claude Chappe invents the first long-distance semaphore (visual or optical) telegraph line.
1814	Joseph Nicéphore Niépce achieves the first photographic image.
1821	Charles Wheatstone reproduces sound in a primitive sound box - the first microphone.
1831	Joseph Henry invents the first electric telegraph.
1835	Samuel Morse invents Morse code.
1843	Samuel Morse invents the first long distance electric telegraph line. Alexander Bain patents the first fax machine.
1861	United States starts the Pony Express for mail delivery. Coleman Sellers invents the Kinematoscope - a machine that flashed a series of still photographs onto a screen.
1876	Thomas Edison patents the mimeograph - an office copying machine. Alexander Graham Bell patents the electric telephone. Melvyl Dewey writes the Dewey Decimal System for ordering library books.
1877	Thomas Edison patents the phonograph with a wax cylinder as recording medium. Eadweard Muybridge invents high speed photography creating first moving pictures that captured motion.
1887	Emile Berliner invents the gramophone - a system of recording which could be used over and over again.
1888	George Eastman patents Kodak roll film camera.
1889	Almon Strowger patents the direct dial telephone or automatic telephone exchange.
1894	Guglielmo Marconi improves wireless telegraphy.

1898	First telephone answering machines.
1899	Valdemar Poulsen invents the first magnetic recordings - using magnetized steel tape as recording medium - the foundation for both mass data storage on disk and tape and the music recording industry. Loudspeakers invented.
1902	Guglielmo Marconi transmits radio signals from Cornwall to Newfoundland - the first radio signal across the Atlantic Ocean.
1904	First regular comic books.
1906	Lee Deforest invents the electronic amplifying tube or triode - this allowed all electronic signals to be amplified improving all electronic communications i.e. telephones and radios.
1910	Thomas Edison demonstrated the first talking motion picture.
1914	First cross continental telephone call made.
1916	First radios with tuners - different stations.
1923	The television or iconoscope (cathode-ray tube) invented by Vladimir Kosma Zworykin - first television camera.
1925	John Logie Baird transmits the first experimental television signal.
1926	Warner Brothers Studios invented a way to record sound separately from the film on large disks and synchronized the sound and motion picture tracks upon playback - an improvement on Thomas Edison's work.
1927	NBC starts two radio networks. CBS founded. First television broadcasts in England. Warner Brothers releases "The Jazz Singer" the first successful talking motion picture.
1930	Radio popularity spreads with the "Golden Age" of radio. First television broadcasts in the United States. Movietone system of recording film sound on an audio track right on the film invented.
1934	Joseph Begun invents the first tape recorder for broadcasting - first magnetic recording.
1938	Television broadcasts able to be taped and edited - rather than only live.
1939	Scheduled television broadcasts begin.
1944	Computers like Harvard's Mark I put into public service - government owned - the age of Information Science begins.
1947	First discovery of Dead Sea Scrolls (continued through 1956)
1948	Long playing record invented - vinyl and played at 33 rpm. Transistor invented - enabling the miniaturization of electronic devices.
1949	Network television starts in U.S.. 45 rpm record invented.
1951	Computers are first sold commercially.

1958	Chester Carlson invents the photocopier or Xerox machine. Integrated Circuit invented - enabling the further miniaturization of electronic devices and computers.
1963	Zip codes invented in the United States.
1966	Xerox invents the Telecopier - the first successful fax machine.
1969	ARPANET - the first Internet started.
1971	The computer floppy disc invented. The microprocessor invented - considered a computer on a chip.
1972	HBO invents pay-TV service for cable.
1973	The "New International Version" Bible
1976	Apple I home computer invented. First nationwide programming via satellite by Ted Turner.
1979	First cellular phone communication network started in Japan..
1980	Sony Walkman invented.
1981	Philips demonstrates first audio Compact Disc
1981	IBM PC first sold. First laptop computers sold to public. Computer mouse becomes regular part of computer.
1983	Time magazines names the computer as "Man of the Year." First cellular phone network started in the United States.
1984	Apple Macintosh released. IBM PC AT released.
1985	Cellular telephones in cars become wide-spread. CD-ROMs in computers.
1994	American government releases control of internet and WWW is born - making communication at lightspeed.
1996	FCC approval of High Definition television specification
1997	Introduction of DVDs and players
1999	Launch of Napster file sharing service (notable for illegal music sharing and downloading)
2001	Apple introduces first iPod
2004	Launch of MySpace
2004	Launch of Facebook
2007	Introduction of iPhone
2007	Presidential debates on YouTube
2008	Barack Obama Elected President in large part from use of Internet-based resources
2010	Introduction of iPad

http://inventors.about.com/library/inventors/bl_history_of_communication.htm

http://www.computerhistory.org/timeline/

http://www.popsci.com/bown/2009

CHAPTER FOUR
What is Web 2.0?

To understand Web 2.0, a better question might be, "What was Web 1.0?" If you have been using the Internet for more than 15 years, you probably remember a time when Web browsers were very basic. You only had text and a few images or graphics, but nothing coming close to what we see today with video, audio, interactive graphics, and much more. I remember using a service called CompuServe that did not use a web browser, only a computer screen that showed plain white text on a black background, with no graphics or icons. CompuServe was sort of an online community, without any rich content, that allowed you to research various topics, retrieve scores of sporting events, stock prices, read news headlines and access other information resources. When Netscape introduced its Web browser in 1994, the Internet began to feel more like a useful tool and less like an oddity.

The term "Web 2.0" emerged from a brainstorming session conducted by Tim O'Reilly and Dale Dougherty *(oreilly. com/web2/archive/what-is-web-20.html)*. These discussions led to the first annual Web 2.0 conference in 2004, which is widely recognized as the authority on all things Web 2.0. There is also some disagreement regarding the precise definition of Web 2.0, ranging from a genuine paradigm shift to a trendy "buzzword." O'Reilly offers the following compact definition of Web. 2.0:

Web 2.0 is the network as platform, spanning all connected devices; Web 2.0 applications are those that make the most of the intrinsic advantages of that platform: delivering software as a continually-updated service that gets better the more people use it, consuming and remixing data from multiple sources, including individual users, while providing their own data and services in a form that allows remixing by others, creating network effects through an "architecture of participation," and going beyond the page metaphor of Web 1.0 to deliver rich user experiences. (radar.oreilly.com/archives/2005/10/web-20-compact-definition.html)

Web 2.0 capabilities resulted from faster Internet speeds, increased bandwidth of Internet connections and a host of other advancements in hardware, processing power, Internet protocols, vastly improved servers and software.

If you have ever used Wikipedia to read information posted by other users like yourself, you have experienced Web 2.0. If you have ever left a comment on a blog, you were experiencing Web 2.0. If you have had the opportunity to do a live video chat with someone across the nation or on the other side of the world using Skype, you experienced the full capability of Web 2.0. There are web-based applications today that will provide virtual tours of homes, custom configurations of automobiles, online dressing rooms that allow a "virtual you" to try on different styles and colors of clothes. Online shopping and banking are other Web 2.0 type functions.

Web 2.0 is not an application that was invented and owned by an individual or company. It is a set of capabilities and web services which have all been made possible by increased Internet bandwidth, improved protocols, and the ingenuity of developers. Web 2.0 applications are becoming increasingly sophisticated. Google has introduced applications such as word processing, spreadsheets, and contact management. In March of 2008, Adobe introduced a web-based version of Photoshop. All of these sophisticated applications are supported by both increased bandwidth and improved Internet protocols. In addition to needing to have a fast Internet connection, it is also necessary to own a computer that is capable of processing "client-side" data and instructions. In the world of Web 2.0, there is both a "server-side" and a "client-side." Server side refers to those processes that occur within the computer (the server) that is serving up the Web 2.0 application to you. Client-side refers to those processes that are handed off to your computer (the client) from the Web 2.0 application. Even with a very fast Internet connection, it would not be possible to edit an image using the online version of Photoshop if all the processing occurred server-side and updated in real time over your Internet connection. A lot of these applications load the data and instructions into the memory of your computer for processing. The results are saved back to the server, or the "cloud" (*See Chapter Eight to learn more about cloud computing*).

Web 2.0 applications require a full time connection to the Internet to be useful beyond the desktop. Mobile devices such as iPhones, iPads, and cellular Internet connected tablet PCs, have that full time connection.

Pastors, ministry leaders and others who are unable to work from an office will find great benefit using Web 2.0 technology.

 To see a list of Web 2.0 Internet-based applications, visit the companion website.

PART TWO: Strategic Thinking

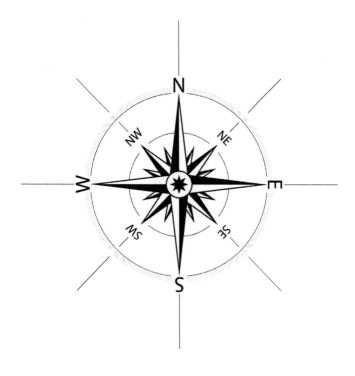

CHAPTER FIVE
Strategic and Tactical Uses for Media and New Media in Ministry

New media extends the usefulness of live presentations such as sermons and performances. Before the advent of the printing press and later audio/video recording devices, any live presentation only benefited those who had the good fortune to be present. Today, we can hardly conceive of a great speech or musical performance being unavailable for later enjoyment. In times past, such occasions where lost to persons not present. Jesus' great sermons and miracles were performed in the presence of people. Bible writers such as Matthew, Mark Luke and John recorded their versions of events under the inspiration of God. Only heaven's record will tell the full story of all the great things that happened that were not recorded in the Scriptures. John 21:25 says, *"And there are also many other things that Jesus did, which if they were written one by one, I suppose that even the world itself could not contain the books that would be written."*

The Utility of New Media

One of the great benefits of media and new media is the capability to preserve a performance for later playback or consumption. This is something we take for granted today with our Digital Video Recorders (DVRs) and TiVo devices. Churches routinely record the pastor's message for distribution on Compact Disc or digital download over the Internet. Some ministries can also provide standard and high definition video recordings of church meetings for broadcast, webcast or DVD distribution.

New Media Strategy and Tactics

As a technology of media convergence, new media offers 21st Century churches many modes of communication of life enhancing and life changing information. With access to an ever-increasing host of technologies, tools and techniques, it is essential to be more purpose and mission driven, than device/gadget-driven. Without the guiding outline of a clear mission, as a strategy, it is too easy to become overwhelmed by an abundance of new media resources and tactics.

Strategic defined: *Relating to the identification of long-term or overall aims and interests and the means of achieving*

Tactical defined: *Done or for use in immediate support of an operation.*

During times of armed conflict, commanders must first clarify strategic objectives before committing to specific tactics such as sending troops into harms' way, or dropping bombs. For a ministry, only desiring to have the "latest and greatest" computers and equipment will only guarantee that money is spent. Having gear cannot guarantee any effectiveness related to the mission of the church.

The many uses of new media offers virtually endless possibilities for tactical effectiveness in ministry. However, finding effectiveness requires some level of strategic planning. The concept of a strategic plan seems daunting. However, we are not talking about developing a strategic plan for the whole ministry. We are talking about developing a new media related strategy around specific purposes or objectives provided by ministry leadership. These strategies are smaller in scale, but no less important, within the context of the media ministry of the church.

For example: A church Young Adult Ministry's summer plan calls for engaging young adults in the wholesome use of social media networks like Facebook for outreach to their friends. In response, the church's the Media Team can act either *strategically* or *tactically.* One tactic might involve creating a video commercial promoting the Facebook outreach. Using a tactical approach, without thinking strategically, is how we usually approach new projects. Create something that seems to "fit."

Let's assume that the video promo is produced and is shown on the big screen during the church service and on the church website. What is the next step: Show the video again and again?

Taking a strategic approach to the young adult outreach project might begin by asking good questions:

1. Where does this outreach fit within the larger vision of the ministry?

2. What are the objectives for this young adult outreach? (See the next chapter on "The Power of Good Objectives" to know the definition of an objective.)

3. What is the time frame for this outreach?

4. Who are the key young adults and leaders in our ministry best qualified to lead this effort?

5. What types and frequency of media would best serve this purpose?

When objectives are identified, the media team can much more effectively select the best tools and tactics.

Given the information gained from a strategic approach, the media team may determine that three videos are needed, to include "man on the street" candid content. They may determine to schedule the release of video to coincide with a major event in the city. They may decide to coordinate with graphic designers who will develop a special logo, posters, flyers or direct mail items using similar themes. The pastor may also agree to preach a special message to support the outreach.

All of the above *tactics* are informed more by *strategic thinking* and planning. This approach is better than simply creating and showing a video, or having the graphics person working separately to create a flyer outside of a strategic plan of action.

CHAPTER SIX
The Power of Clear Objectives

"For if the trumpet give an uncertain sound, who shall prepare himself to the battle?" (I Corinthians 14:8, KJV)

Why Purposes Don't Prosper

Without clear objectives, we cannot expect good outcomes. Tools and tactics need a strategy just like wood, hammers, nails, and carpenters need a blueprint of the construction plan. Disappointing results often come from unclear, unmeasurable objectives or a lack of an overall strategy. Everyone has his or her own understanding of an objective. The common definition is: "A thing aimed at or sought." This definition is the same as a "goal."

The best understanding of using objectives comes from the domain of instructional design and education. **An objective is:** *A statement of expectation of what behavior persons will be able to demonstrate after learning, training, or involvement in a program.*

Example of poorly formed objectives:

If the program goal was training people how to use a telephone, the objective might read:

"After completing this training you will be able to...:"

1. operate your phone

2. know how to greet callers

3. understand the procedure for transferring a call

On the surface, this looks good. This is the type of objective statement that we usually write. However, here's the problem with this example: These objectives do not indicate behaviors that can be observed and assessed. How does this statement indicate if the person knows or understands something? What does it really mean to operate the phone?

Example of well formed objectives that includes observable behaviors.

"After completing this training you will be able to...

1. place a caller on hold

2. activate the speaker phone

3. play new messages on the voice mail system

4. list the three elements of a proper phone greeting

5. transfer a call to a requested extension

These objectives are developed around specific tasks. Instead of the vague objective to "operate the phone," the trainee knows exactly what is expected for successfully operating the telephone. We can observe the person activating the speaker phone, checking voice mail, or extending a good greeting to callers. A well formed objective avoids vague verbs such as "understand," "know," or "learn about." It is better to use verbs (action words).

Better words to use with objectives are shown following the statement: *"At the conclusion of this lesson, program, outreach, etc., you will be able to..."* list, identify, state, describe, define, resolve, compare and contrast, operate (specifically)"

Let's apply this understanding of objectives to the Facebook Outreach project example we used earlier.

First, here's an example of a poorly formed objective:

"The Facebook outreach for young adults will help young adults of Christ Christian Church to connect with their peers on Facebook. We will influence unsaved and unchurched young adults to follow Christ and visit our church."

This is actually more of a *goal statement*. Goals are important, but you cannot build a program or a media strategy around goals alone.

Example of well formed objectives:

"When our Facebook outreach is complete in 60 days, persons we have reached will be able to..."

1. identify the people who have reached out to them

2. contact their Facebook friends and invite them in to our church FB group

3. describe how to come to faith in Jesus Christ

4. download the latest Podcast from Pastor Bob

5. sign up online for one of our scheduled seminars

This example offers more concrete action items. Each statement begins with a verb describing an action that can be observed and assessed.

Ministry leaders and the media team will do much better planning and production with clear objectives in mind. Another benefit of having good objectives is that it will be easier to look back following the program to determine if objectives were met, or why they were not met.

CHAPTER SEVEN
Have You Met "ADDIE?"

Strategic thinking involves many techniques for considering how best to reach people for Christ, address spiritual conditions that negatively affect them, and effectively serve our congregations. Strategic thinking also considers how we may continue to be relevant and effective in an uncertain future.

Designing Effective Solutions

I learned about the ADDIE development model during my Masters degree program in Instructional Systems Technology at Indiana University, Bloomington. ADDIE is a well known and time tested development model among instructional designers who help people learn and increase levels of performance and productivity among all types of learners. The ADDIE model is used in the development of curriculum and learning materials at every level. ADDIE is also an excellent process model for many other types of development, including media and ministry projects.

A.D.D.I.E. is an acronym for:

Analysis

Design

Development

Implementation

Evaluation

Analysis

Analysis begins with observing and talking to the people currently being served as well as those whom you would like to reach. We should also seek to understand the culture and conditions that shape their lives. It is about asking good questions, listening closely to the answers, and most importantly, not making assumptions about people or their culture. It is always a humbling experience to have made assumptions about people, only to discover, upon deeper inquiry, that our assumptions were false. It is far better to take the time to listen and gather information about people based on their responses and felt needs. Questionnaires are sometimes useful during this phase.

The analysis phase is an information gathering stage and an opportunity to open your mind and heart to people you want to serve. If we spend quality time with people within their environments, we'll begin to understand their needs and potential. Listening and learning helps us develop realistic strategies.

Design

The design stage takes the information gathered from the analysis stage to help design a teaching, training program, outreach, new media project or whatever is needed to meet the needs that have been revealed from the analysis stage. A lot of prayer and thinking go into good design. During this phase, also draw upon examples from other ministries and research materials. The design stage is also an ideal time to use resources that you have gained from educational experiences, from books, from materials and knowledge gained at seminars and workshops you have attended.

The key is to draw upon *all needed resources* to design a good program or project.

The main goal of the design stage is to create objectives

that will guide the remainder of the process and keep everything in focus. Refer back to Chapter Six, "*The Power of Good Objectives*," to gain a clear understanding of the importance of well crafted objectives. Without clear, measurable objectives, the design process will break down during the next three stages.

Good design also considers the roles of team members in the process. We determine what skills are needed and we look within the ministry for persons who possess those needed skills. Sometimes it is necessary to go outside the ministry to partner with other churches. The program or project may require the use of consultants or paid professionals.

One of the key steps in the design phase is to "count the cost" of the endeavor. Needed materials, expenses and expected income (if warranted) should all be carefully considered and compiled into a budget.

The final step in the design process is to produce a document that outlines the entire program and project. This "Design Document" or proposal can be very persuasive, especially when a presentation is needed to secure approval and funding.

Development

The development stage is where the actual work begins. Development involves meeting with team members and making expenditures, as outlined in the design document and budget. Depending on the type of project being developed and the objectives for that project, Bible lessons are written, meetings scheduled, video scripts are drafted, support people are recruited, special web pages or flyers are created, and whatever is necessary to fulfill the design plan.

During this stage, all team members should have the design document in hand. In the words of Habakkuk, the "vision" is "made plain" in writing so that everyone knows their roles and are working together as a team.

In many churches and organizations, the development stage is *where we usually begin* working on ministry projects.

However, important projects should begin with analysis and design on some level.

Implementation

The implementation stage is the point at which the program or project is done. The outreach is conducted. The conference is on. The video is shown. The performance takes place. Everything that was developed is now on display and in use. People are being blessed and God is glorified! Said another way, *now the fun begins!* The quality of the program or project is the public evidence of the many hours of prayer, planning and preparation.

Evaluation

The final stage in the ADDIE model is evaluation. Evaluation involves assessing the quality and effectiveness of the program or project. This is also the time where the clarity of the objectives greatly help in measuring success. Again, if you have not done so, read Chapter Six, *The Power of Good Objectives*, to appreciate the importance of comparing objectives to the actual outcomes of teaching, training program, outreach, new media project or whatever the purpose of the original plan.

The ADDIE development model can be used formally or informally. It is applicable in some form to almost any type of ministry program or project.

Application & Action

 Below are two brief questionnaires that may aid in understanding individual or organization patterns and predispositions that may impact strategic thinking. *[Retrieved June 22, 2010 from Slideshare.net presentation, http://bit.ly/b6SoYX]*

Indicate your or your department's tendency in this area:

Trying to rush the process:

[ ] Never, [ ] Sometimes, [ ] Often

Not being flexible to change how you think/change tools:

[ ] Never, [ ] Sometimes, [ ] Often

Falling in love with the tools:

[ ] Never, [ ] Sometimes, [ ] Often

Too much emphasis on form instead of function:

[ ] Never, [ ] Sometimes, [ ] Often

Not willing to ask for help or pay for advice and expertise:

[ ] Never, [ ] Sometimes, [ ] Often

Keep trying to make old thing work, rather than investing better tools:

[ ] Never, [ ] Sometimes, [ ] Often

Understanding Your Organization's Online Culture

What does our website communicate about us?:

[ ] Never thought about it, [ ] Have thought about it, [ ] Greatly concerned

What are the unspoken cultural cues we're using?:

[ ] Never thought about it, [ ] Have thought about it, [ ] Greatly concerned

What does our language say about us?:

[ ] Never thought about it, [ ] Have thought about it, [ ] Greatly concerned

Does our digital culture match our physical culture?:

[ ] Never thought about it, [ ] Have thought about it, [ ] Greatly concerned

Are we attracting or repelling users?:

[ ] Never thought about it, [ ] Have thought about it, [ ] Greatly concerned

Is our website optimized for search engines like Google?:

[ ] Never thought about it, [ ] Have thought about it, [ ] Greatly concerned

PART THREE: Getting Things Done

CHAPTER EIGHT
Finding Your Productivity Sweet Spot

The term "sweet spot" comes from sports like tennis and golf. As a golfer, I've had the good experience of striking the golf ball with the center, or sweet spot of the golf club. When this happens, the stroke feels almost effortless because this part of the golf club was designed to provide the best action on the ball.

In our work for the Lord, we have "sweet spots" where His grace and our efforts meet. We want, and need, to find better methods for working and getting things done. Exploring productivity tools and techniques is one way of working "smarter" and not only "harder."

Saving time and money are always important goals for individuals and organizations. In the 21st century, new media can play an important role in helping us become more productive personally and organizationally.

In this chapter, we will examine some of the tools and concepts for being more productive and efficient, which will translate into saving money and time.

One of the great challenges pastors and church leaders face today is dealing with the deluge of information that comes in the form of telephone calls, e-mails, requests for meetings, documents that need to be reviewed, managing accounts, and overseeing various ministries and processes. While there are no shortcuts to high quality, there are methods and technologies that can make the workload easier and more satisfying.

Over the years, we have seen changing platforms for managing our time and projects. In the 1980's and earlier, everyone used paper-based systems such as DayTimer and Franklin. In the 1990s, we began to see the emergence of desktop computers. Large organizations could afford to install dedicated servers with customized software to support database operations for the Local Area Network (LAN). However, these systems were of little use to individuals working away from the office network.

The emergence of the Internet and laptop computers in the early 1990s, along with the coming of devices such as the Palm personal digital assistant, or PDA, began to allow individuals to become more mobile and less dependent on paper for personal project organization. By the year 2000, paper-based systems were all but discarded for those who could afford laptop computers and mobile devices like the now obsolete Palm.

Today, it is rare to see someone carrying a DayTimer or Franklin planner. Most leaders carry a Windows or Macintosh laptop computer. Many also carry a smart phone such as Blackberry, iPhone, or an Android device. As of this writing, it appears that the Apple iPad may lead a resurgence of tablet computing.

One of the latest new media-based technologies to support personal and organizational productivity is something called "cloud computing." Just as we used to speak about the importance of broadband Internet access or high speed Internet connections, the concept of cloud computing is becoming commonplace today.

Are you in the Cloud?

What is the cloud? The cloud is another one of the innovations of the Web 2.0 revolution. The cloud is a buzzword that describes networked computers and storage space available to individual users over the Internet. The cloud concept and online applications are not new. Since Internet speeds have greatly increased for everyday users, and powerful mobile devices have emerged, storing data and running applications entirely over the Internet have become practical.

More importantly, we have grown increasingly comfortable with the concept of storing data and information on Internet servers and not only within our computers. The concept of cloud computing can be understood by the following examples:

1. Web-based e-mail is the most commonly used cloud application. If you use services such as Yahoo or Gmail for e-mail, you know that you must log in to your account using an Internet connected web browser to access your e-mail. People who use hard drive based e-mail software such as Outlook or Apple Mail know that their e-mail is stored on their hard drives, as well as in the cloud.

2. Online stock trading and banking are other examples of cloud computing. Many banks no longer send account statements by postal mail. All the information that is needed is available in the cloud and accessible via web browsers such as Firefox or Internet Explorer. There are also dedicated banking applications for mobile devices like iPhone. Business can be transacted online while on the move.

3. Coordinating calendars and event collaboration among team members living in different cities represent an ideal use of cloud computing. Solutions such as Microsoft Exchange Server have provided collaboration tools for many years, but at a very steep cost. One of the best free cloud computing solutions is hosted by Google. (More about Google apps below)

4. The cloud enables online backup of data. Some or all of the information stored on hard drives can be automatically backed up to the cloud if you have a full time, and fast, Internet connection.

Recommended Cloud-Based Productivity Applications

There are a great number of applications that rely on the cloud for functionality. Some of these applications, like Skype, are installed on hard drives, yet are only useful when connected to the Internet. Everyone has their favorites. Below is a list of selected apps that I have found productive.

Visit *www.newmediaforministry.com/book* to share your recommendations and reviews of cloud applications

1. **Jott** (*Jott.com*) voice memo system. Converts your voice memo to text that is automatically e-mailed or sent via SMS to the recipient of your choosing. Can also post dates and voice to Google Calendar. Monthly fee.

2. **If By Phone** (*ifbyphone.com*) You call the system from your phone, leave a message, and your message is sent to a predefined set of recipients. Manage your lists and view call reports online. Monthly fee.

3. **Skype** (*Skype.com*) Skype is a desktop application that uses the Internet for audio or video chat sessions using your webcam or built in microphone to make calls to other computers or telephones. Great solution for international calls, especially when using Skype on both ends. Fee for making calls to telephone. Free for Skype to Skype calls.

4. **Dropbox** (*Dropbox.com*). Powerful file sharing and storage system. If you have DropBox installed on all your computers and mobile devices, any file added or edited will be synced and appear on every device. Changes made to documents appear on all devices that share an account. Free for up to 2GB.

5. **Evernote** (*Evernote.com*). Evernote works in a similar manner as DropBox, but is based on the storage and synchronization of notes and web links across all of your devices that share the same account. Stored PDFs are converted to a searchable document. Free.

6. **Logmein** (*logmein.com*) Remote access software can sometime be an indispensable tool, especially when there is the

need to start or manage processes on computers at the office or home. Other products include Timbuktu and GoToMyPC. Logmein is free for typical service levels.

7. **DragonDictate** mobile app (*Nuance.com*) Works like the desktop Dragon Naturally Speaking or MacSpeech application, except that the processing and translation take place in the cloud. Results are returned to your mobile device. Free app.

8. **FedexOffice** (*fedex.com/us/office*) The former Kinkos franchise offers remote printing tools that allow uploading of documents, booklets, flyers, posters, etc., that can be ordered and picked at any FedEx Office center.

9. **Google Apps** (*Google.com*) Google is known for its search engine. The enormous revenue made from advertising has allowed Google to develop many free as well as enterprise-level applications and services. Among the most useful Google properties are Documents (Word processing), Sites (simple web development), Groups (Collaboration tool), Calendar, Picasa (For photo storage and sharing), Gmail (e-mail), Blogger (for blogs), and Google Voice (Voice Over IP and voicemail solution that includes a unique telephone number). These tools are as useful as they are powerful.

10. **Bible study and research tools** such as *BibleGateway.com, YouVersion.com* and *BlueLetterBible.org*. Free.

11. **Online database applications** help manage membership information. These solutions offer a wide range of functionality from simple and inexpensive, like Zoho (*Zoho.com*), to complex and expensive, like Zondervan's "The City " (*Onthecity.org*)

12. **Flickr** (flickr.com) A Yahoo product that offers great utitlity for storing and sharing photos, metadata (data about the image and camera settings), and control over viewing. The paid account offers virtually unlimited storage of images.

13. **Twitter** (*twitter.com*) Twitter comes under the social network category, but has become a unique service if wisely used. Twitter messages are limited to 140 characters, so all posts are concise. If you only follow people who offer useful and important information or insights, Twitter will be a valuable resource. Equally, it is good to use Twitter to share your insightful updates, which may garner your own following.

14. **Personal and project managers such as Basecamp** (*basecamphq.com*), OmniFocus (*Omnigroup.com*), CarbonFin Outliner (*carbonfin.com*) and many, many more. Free or Monthly fee.

15. **MobileMe** (mobileme.com) For Macintosh and Windows Users, Apple's MobileMe offers an excellent suite of integrated cloud-based utilities. While Google has many of the same features for free, The User Interface (UI) and integration with Apple devices is highly usable. Annual fee for MobileMe account.

16. **Social networks** such as Facebook are useful for connecting with constituents, friends and acquaintances. Everything one needs to know about Facebook can be found with a simple Google search. Services like Myspace are too often replete with gaudiness and self-promotion to be useful for ministry organizations.

 All of these tools (and more online), if used wisely, can increase your personal productivity as well as become time and money savers. As pastors and ministry leaders, these tools can also become aids to collaboration and staying connected with parishioners, colleagues, and with the larger community of believers in Christ.

CHAPTER NINE
Getting into the Flow

Getting to a "flow state" is something of which preachers and performers are familiar. We know that the Holy Spirit empowers us for godly purposes. We should also recognize that there are physical and mental aspects to getting into the flow of your work.

Most of the content for this chapter is taken from the book, *The Power of Less* by Leo Babauta. While this is not a biblically based book, Mr. Babauta challenges our common views about time management and getting things done. This excerpt is from Chapter Nine of *The Power of Less:*

Simple Time Management

Immersing yourself in a task, completely, is a phenomenon called "flow." Flow has gotten a lot of attention recently, in both the scientific world and the world of productivity, because people have discovered that the state of flow can lead to increased productivity and happiness. Basically, flow is a state of mind that occurs when you lose yourself in a task, and the world around you disappears. You lose track of time. We've all experienced this from time to time-the trick is learning how to purposefully get yourself into flow. The way to get into flow:

1. Choose a task you're passionate about. If it's something you don't care about, you won't find flow.

2. Choose a task that's challenging. But not too challenging-if it's too difficult, you'll have a hard time getting into flow. If it's too easy, you'll get bored.

3. Eliminate distractions. The less you think about other things, the better. You want to focus completely on this task. Get rid of distractions such as phones, e-mail notifications, instant-messaging, clutter on your desk or computer desktop, etc.

4. Immerse yourself in the task. Just start on the task, and focus completely on it. Forget about everything else, and let the world melt away. Get excited about the task and have fun. Warning: You may lose track of time and be late for your next appointment-which is why it's a bad idea to schedule too many appointments.

KNOW YOUR PRIORITIES

If you have an open schedule, how do you know what you should be working on at any given moment? Priorities. See the last chapter on Most Important Tasks (MITs)-basically, you should decide first thing in the morning what you want to accomplish each day.

Make a short list of three things you'd really like to accomplish. Your three most important things. You can have a short list of other small tasks you'd like to do in a batch (save them for later in the day), but the focus of your day should be the list of three important things. Let this list, and not your schedule, be the ruler of your day.

Once you've set your priorities, the trick is finding focus. I highly recommend that you focus on one thing at a time. To get your short list of three important tasks completed, you'll need to focus on each one of those tasks in turn, and try to focus on them to completion. This will also be a radical departure for the multi-tasker in all of us.

But single-tasking is not only more productive, it's more relaxing as well. It will take a little while for you to get used to single-tasking, if you are used to jumping from one thing to another and back. That's OK. Just gently bring yourself back to your task every time you feel yourself being pulled away. Keep at it and you'll soon be knocking off your most important tasks easily. While you're working on your task, you'll think of other things you need to do, or be interrupted by a coworker with a request, or an idea will pop into your head. You can't let those ideas and requests rule your life. Instead of switching tasks, just make a note of other tasks or ideas as they come up, to consider for later. Have a sheet of paper or a small notebook or a text 'file on your computer (or wherever you write your list of three important tasks), and get back to the task you were working on. When you're done with that task, you can take a look at your list to see what you should be working on next.

 (Learn more about *The Power of Less* at, www.the-powerofless.com)

Redeem the Time: Make the Most of Every Opportunity

Media production is very time intensive. This is something not understood by persons who have not done production work. Managing both time and projects is crucial. We want to always prioritize time with the Lord, with family and friends, so being a little ruthless with everything (but never with people) is necessary. Below are some scriptures to consider in light of dealing with time and responsibilities.

See then that you walk circumspectly, not as fools but as wise, redeeming the time, because the days are evil. Therefore do not be unwise, but understand what the will of the Lord is. Ephesians 5:15-17

Therefore, when I was planning this, did I do it lightly? Or the things I plan, do I plan according to the flesh, that with me there should be Yes, Yes, and No, No? 2 Cor. 1:17,

And He has made from one blood every nation of men to dwell on all the face of the earth, and has determined their pre-appointed times and the boundaries of their habitation, Acts 17:26

The plans of the diligent lead surely to plenty, but those of everyone who is hasty, surely to poverty. Prov. 21:5

The counsel of the LORD stands forever, The plans of His heart to all generations. Psalm 33:11

Problems Produced by a Lack of Time Management:

1. Open ended dreams and visions
2. Unfulfilled obligations
3. Items done other than stated goals and purposes
4. Lack of order which produces an invasion into personal and family time
5. Sense of bewilderment or lack of focus
6. Reacting to circumstances rather than responding to a plan
7. Lack of excellence in duties performed
8. Missed opportunities

Time Wasters to Avoid:

1. Unproductive telephone conversations
2. Excess leisure which produces laziness
3. Long meetings and/or conversations (scheduled or unscheduled)
4. Lack of proper supplies/materials on hand
5. Unscheduled or unexpected visits and stops

6. Lack of delegation

7. Mistakes in procedure or use that must be corrected later

8. Waiting for people or things

9. Multiple trips to the same place for separate items

10. Delaying decisions

11. Answering the same questions

12. "Not Watching the Monkey." If you value your time in managing projects, remember to *"Watch the Monkey:"* The "monkey" is the responsibility carried by another person who wants to transfer it to you. *Don't let the monkey jump!*

13. Trying to help people that you cannot help or solve problems you cannot solve

14. Small talk when business is at hand

CHAPTER TEN
How to Hire Help

Strategic thinking can help in the process of knowing when to hire expertise. Being clear about objectives provides the best basis for selecting the tools and tactics for a project. Ministries are inherently focused on saving money and finding value when investing limited financial resources. We all know the lessons of going cheap and regretting the results. We also know the pain of overpaying for goods and services. Both extremes should be avoided, but not for fear of either extreme.

If you have been burned by paying too much for a service that under-performed, the temptation is to resist paying more even when it is necessary. If you have been burned by purchasing a low cost/low quality service that was nearly unusable, you must resist the temptation of thinking that simply paying more will bring greater value. Value comes from goods and services that exceed our expectations regardless of cost. Generally, the cheapest good or service will not succeed in exceeding our expectations.

Questions to Ask Before You Hire

When deciding when to hire a professional individual or firm, consider the following questions:

1. Is there anyone within my organization that can deliver the quality I expect within the time frame needed?

2. If I use a volunteer, will I be bound to accept whatever product he delivers? Can this person accept constructive criticism and improve the product without feeling that I am being ungrateful for not accepting his first submission?

3. Do I need goods and services that rival the quality of similar items outside the church?

4. Will the product or service hold up over time? Does the investment justify the time frame in which the product or service will be used?

5. Can I find peace of mind after committing a project to a staff member or volunteer within the organization?

6. If I choose a staff member or volunteer who has lesser skills than a professional, can I live with the results and be content if the product is less in quality than I expected?

Understanding fair pricing and fees is important to getting projects done that require outside help, while at the same time working within your budget. Some considerations when pricing services include:

1. What is the current market rate for the good or service that I seek?

2. Will my perspective contractor be willing to work below market rate?

3. Is there a talented and capable person within our organization that can be developed and trained to provide needed services as a staff person? Will our future workload justify this investment?

4. What is the difference in quality and value between the low, middle and high bidders?

5. Is the perspective contractor responsive to telephone calls and e-mails? If a perspective contractor is slow to return phone calls and e-mails, it is unlikely that communications will improve after hiring.

6. Am I satisfied that the bid thoroughly explains the terms of the services to be rendered? Have my questions been an-

swered?

7. What is the track record of the contractor? What do others say about their work?

8. Am I pleased with the previous work performed for other clients?

These are a few considerations that go into choosing to hire expertise. It is best to develop a relationship that can grow over time. Often, consistent customers receive discounts for services as well as prioritization when deadlines are looming.

The old saying is still true: *"You get what you pay for."*

CHAPTER ELEVEN
Internet Safety & Security

Any discussion about new media and the Internet would be incomplete without exploring the issue of Internet safety and security. As we are all aware, there are a host of perils associated with using the Internet and new media. The Internet is a wealth of information and content of all types. It is both a gold mine and a cesspool. Internet services that we bring into our offices and homes bring us life enhancing information. The Internet can also deliver the equivalent of a "Trojan Horse," which, like the ancient story was a kind of ambush disguised as a gift and allowed entry into a fortified place. As the story goes, after nightfall, a door opened from the bottom of the Trojan horse, and out came the enemy to wreak havoc.

Internet safety and decency are concerns that all believers in Christ, churches, and responsible organizations should share. We all remember horror stories like the 1999 Columbine, Colorado massacre in which the youthful perpetrators used the Internet to gather and share information in developing their plot for mass murder. We know that people have used the Internet to learn how to make bombs. Terrorists use online resources to devise wicked plans for destruction. Pornographers and sexual predators use the Internet to prey upon children and morally weak people.

We should be vigilant and proactive in taking a stand for

the sake of our children and the overall good of our churches and community.

Supervising Internet Usage

Parents, teachers, church leaders, etc., should determine the level of responsibility and freedom afforded to persons who use computers they do not own. Unfettered access to the Internet is as much a risk factor as "latch key" children who come home to empty houses after school.

Tactics for Godly Internet Use

From a biblical perspective, we understand the power of temptation as well as the power of accountability. When a person knows that he will be held accountable for his actions, his whereabouts and deeds, he is more likely to resist temptation if there is a risk of exposure for misdeeds. It is not so much motivation by fear, as it is recognition of sinful human nature.

1. For children and teens, computers connected to the Internet should be located *in the open*. Remote access and keystroke recording software should be installed. Tell your children that you intend to monitor activity on computers in your house.

2. Develop a policy for Internet usage on computers used at the church. Post your policy where computers are used. Install software to block access to pornography, and that also will report attempts to break the filters.

3. Configure computers to disable Internet access or turn themselves off during the time when people should be sleeping.

4. To avoid computer viruses and other cyber-attacks, instruct people not to open e-mail from unknown persons or click on attachments.

5. For better security, consider using Macintosh computers for public access on your network. These systems are immune to viruses, worms, and every other cyber-attack

designed to affect Windows computers.

Network security

Wireless networks such as WiFi afford a great deal of freedom of movement around one's home or office. Just as all freedom carries a certain level of responsibility, this is also true with respect to computer networks, especially wireless networks. There are two basic types of networks:

1. There is one network type called "LAN" (Local Area Network) that mainly uses a wired (ethernet cable) router to connect computers.

2. There is another network type called "WLAN" (Wireless Local Area Network) that is based mainly on a wireless WiFi network router.

Insofar as outside access is concerned, LANs provide much greater security because the only computers that can access the network must use a physical cable to connect to the network. WLANs are inherently insecure especially when security features are not enabled upon installation. Most people install WiFi routers without consideration for security, which allows anyone within range to access your wireless network. Providing public access to a wireless network is obviously needed under many circumstances, but these networks are set up to separate the public access to the network from critical directories and files on the computer servers.

When seeking to secure your network, don't hesitate to enlist some expert help, whether volunteer or professional in securing your network. While this may be a do-it-yourself project for those who are savvy in using computers and configuring networks, many people still require assistance in securing their networks. If you would like to attempt to secure your network without assistance, there are a host of online resources and specific information from the manufacturer of your wireless router that will guide you through the process of enabling greater security by using passwords.

PART FOUR: Ministering with Media

CHAPTER TWELVE
21st Century Fishers of Men

Mark 1:16 *And as He walked by the Sea of Galilee, He saw Simon and Andrew his brother casting a net into the sea; for they were fishermen. 17 Then Jesus said to them, "Follow Me, and I will make you become fishers of men." 18 They immediately left their nets and followed Him.*

Mark 16:15, *And He said to them, "Go into all the world and preach the gospel to every creature.*

Fishing provides a great analogy for reaching populations for Christ. Fishing is not something that I took seriously. I would put anything on the hook thinking, *"These dumb fish don't know what they are looking at."* Well, I was the dumb one! I learned that fish only want what they like. When I used to go fishing, (I retired since I didn't catch many fish), I would sit out there for hours watching people around me catching fish, while I kept putting bait on my hook and reeling it back empty.

When I had the occasion to go fishing in clear water from a pier, I could observe the behavior of the fish. I noticed that when I presented a poorly baited hook, the fish came close, looked at it, nibbled a little, and then backed off. They could see that my worm was dead or see the exposed hook.

"Fishers of men" must pay attention to what people want and need. We want to design media, ministry and programs that are designed more around what the "fish" want and their environment, than around the presumptions of the fishermen. Chapters 5, 6, & 7 of this book address the importance of *Strategic Thinking* and taking the time to understand the people we want to reach. We don't want to repeat the discredited colonization model practiced by a generation of missionaries in which indigenous people were encouraged to reject their language and culture in favor of adopting a euro-centric or American culture.

We must pray and seek to better understand the people we want to reach. This will allow us a better opportunity to create redemptive relationships that allow us to more persuasively lead people to faith in Christ.

What good fishermen understand

1. **Locate the ideal place to fish.** Some fish are only found in certain waters and at different times of the day and year.

   Application: Go where the people are gathered. Understand their environment.

2. **Select appropriate bait.** Choose the right bait to lure fish. Different kinds of bait are needed to lure different kinds of fish. One size does not fit all.

   Application: Reach people using what is familiar to them without compromising your convictions.

3. **Bait the hook.** Set baits to look as natural as possible and try to disguise the hook.

   Application: People can tell the authentic vs. the fake.

4. **Cast your reel.**

   Application: Go!

5. **Reeling in the fish.** When there is a catch, you have to reel in the fish skillfully to avoid losing it. Do not drag or force it; try to tire the fish before reeling it in completely.

   Application: Love and respect people while gently ministering to them.

These principles can also help us better serve diverse congregations of believers.

CHAPTER THIRTEEN
Using Social Media

The Web 2.0 revolution of the early 2000s spawned the rise of what we now call "social networks." Online communities such as Myspace and Facebook were born among college young adults. As a generation raised among communication technology such as television, mobile phones, and the Internet, it was natural for this generation to develop their paths of communication through these channels. Previous generations communicated in different ways, such as congregating in public places, holding long conversations on landline telephones, and by exchanging letters via postal mail.

Facebook

The generation that came of age at the close of the 20th century used the modes of communication that were most familiar to them. The Internet being the primary mode. In 2004, Mark Zuckerburg and some fellow students at Harvard University started what was originally called, "The Facebook." They developed a web based application for communicating with one another. Facebook was not the first social network of its type and scale. In fact, that distinction belongs to Myspace. While there were certainly other social networks, including AOL-powered instant messaging, in the USA Myspace and Facebook became the most recognizable symbols of this new paradigm of interpersonal communication.

Much has been written about the growth and influence of Facebook. As of June 2010 Facebook boasted an estimated 500 million users! Church leaders and Christians have sought to leverage the power of social networks for the Gospel. Others have encouraged a retreat from the secular social networks in an attempted to form Christian-only networks. But none of these has taken hold on any large scale. I don't think that *socially healthy Christians* are seeking to retreat from society. They are seeking to engage in society while maintaining their convictions, standards and dedication to Christ.

Facebook has become as popular to the Christian community as to the non-Christian community. As with the television, mobile telephone and computer, the vast majority of Christians see no reason not to use social networks. We are not content to stay in the corner and "work our section." Engaging in the larger community is the example that Jesus Christ provided us in the Scriptures. We see that same example of engagement by the early Church in the scriptures.

As we seek to find some transcendent role for Facebook in the context of Kingdom priorities, I have come to the conclusion that Facebook and similar social networks offer about the same value as the telephone, computer, and mobile phone. Facebook is another, howbeit richer, way to communicate. Nothing more, and nothing less. As a means of communication, especially among "friends" whom we actually know, Facebook is a marvelous tool. However, for people who only use Facebook to collect faces and names of people to create a list for promotional purposes, Facebook begins to look like little more than a large mailing list of prospects.

What I also find disappointing is that some Facebook users do not engage in the community. Many only use it as a place to dump feeds from Twitter, endless updates about conditions on *Farmville*, and other less than appealing content for many members. In some ways, Facebook is a social network that is becoming less social.

Ultimately, Facebook may stumble under its own weight as its owners seek to exploit the members by sharing their personal information with advertisers or allowing aggregation of members' interests and preferences for profit.

Twitter

I have found Twitter (Twitter.com) to be a very useful tool. If used thoughtfully, Twitter can provide very focused information from individuals you choose to follow. If you follow people who offer useful and important information or insights, Twitter will be a valuable resource. Equally, it is good to use Twitter to share your insightful posts that may garner followers. My Twitter account (*twitter.com/BryanHudson*) is set up to follow persons who inform my interests in education technology, new media, current events, Macintosh related topics, computer technology news, selected pastors/ministers and some personal friends.

As a "micro-blog," posts made to Twitter, also called "Tweets," are limited to 140 characters. The beauty of this limitation is that updates must be concise and to-the-point. Some of the most useful updates provide a brief summary followed by a web link to the full story or resource.

If you choose to follow hundreds of people, it's essential to create a separate list of your "favorites" so that you can quickly scan their updates. Desktop and mobile software such as *TweetDeck* and *Twitterific* make easy work of managing information from persons you follow.

 If you are interested in learning about Twitter and other social networking utilities, there are numerous "how to" guides online. A Google or YouTube search will yield many useful results. There is also a Twitter tutorial available at *www.newmediaforministry.com/book*

Create You Own Social Network

There are online tools for developing more focused, social networks or online communities. Services such as, *Unifyer* (unifyer.com), *Ning* (ning.com), *Google Groups, The City* (onthecity.org), and *CircleBuilder* (circlebuilder.com) offer this type of service. This service is useful for groups of people, ministries and organizations who require greater control of content and a more focused community experience. This can be a valuable tool for workgroups that require a tighter integration of shared interests.

These services offer a kind of *gated community* for online members. The challenge for these type of services is to attract and hold people who are willing to divide their social media time between Facebook, Twitter, AIM and a private network.

CHAPTER FOURTEEN
New Media Toolbox:
Tools and Tactics for Media Ministry

Once strategies and objectives have been defined, it's time to reach for your Toolbox. I've done a little carpentry with small projects such as building bookcases and doing minor home remodeling. Every project requires a particular set of tools and skills for using those tools. Purchased items that require assembly come with instructions which include a list of the tools needed for proper assembly.

Ministry projects in general, and new media projects in particular require specific tools to get the job done. Along with the tools are the skills needed to effectively use those tools. We'll call these tools and skills, *The Toolbox*. Your *new media toolbox* includes a wide range of ready-to-use resources. It is important to know what tools are available within your ministry. It is also good to invest into tools and skills' training so that when the time comes to get things done, both resources and skilled people are ready to go.

INSIDE THE TOOLBOX

Personnel

Coordinator/Producer: A person responsible to manage a project from beginning to end. Also responsible to select team members, coordinate schedules, and secure needed resources and equipment.

Art Director: Responsible for the artistic value, functional design, and appearance of media products. Leads the team of designers and artists.

Graphic Designer: Develops graphic and image content.

Digital Video producer: Knows how to film using HD video cameras. Can capture and edit digital video using Non Linear editing applications such as Final Cut Pro. Can author DVDs and compress video projects for online distribution.

Web Designer: Understands web development from a technical, artistic, usability, and deployment perspective. Can develop using software tools as well as perform HTML, CSS, and client-side coding. Can incorporate any needed function into the web development process.

Outside Consultant: Firms or individuals hired to perform tasks that are outside the capabilities of ministry staff or volunteers.

Production Assistant: Skilled assistants in particular fields.

Writer/Proofreader: Persons who understand English grammar and style. Can accurately and thoroughly write and edit text.

Promotional Tools

E-mail Blast: An e-mail message sent to multiple persons at once using special software or a service.

Website: The primary online presence for your organization. The public expects every significant organization to have a quality website. People would rather visit online than visit in person.

Flyers: Promotional printed matter that can be distributed by mail, by hand, posted or placed.

Digital Sign: A LCD or Plasma display mounted and used to display videos, messages or announcements.

Press Release: A concise, but descriptive, and well-written document prepared for distribution to traditional and online news outlets. Can be a form of free advertising if deemed news worthy.

Social Networks: An online community such as Facebook and Twitter. Can be a useful promotional tool if properly used. Over-promoting is considered an un-welcomed intrusion among social networks. People who want to become your "friend," only to promote their goods and services are quickly "un-friended." People don't like to be considered the "fish in the barrel" for "easy shooting."

Newsletter: A periodic published document containing news, updates, images and time sensitive content. Can be printed, saved as a PDF or e-mailed.

Senior Leader Blog: A personal web page that catalogs entries by day or easy search and retrieval. A blog is the easiest web based tool to create and maintain.

Webcast / On Demand Video: A live or pre-recorded video or audio web browser based presentation over the Internet using low-end or high-end software and equipment. There are many methods for delivering webcasts and on demand video. (See Chapter 17 for more about video production.)

CDs/DVDs: Easy and inexpensive to duplicate and distribute. DVDs should not be produced using DVD recorders. Computers with special DVD authoring software are the best choice for creating a master DVD.

Banner Ads: Advertising formatted to a standard size and placed on websites for promotional purposes. Banner ads are usually paid forms of advertising.

Google Adwords: A paid service provided by Google in which a Google word search may cause your products and services to appear in the search results.

Video Greeting: A video prepared using a webcam or better camera that is compressed for delivery via e-mail or embedded on a web page.

Brochures: A well designed, high quality printed item that provides information intended to inform and persuade the reader.

Post Cards: A printed card designed for mailing using the discounted Postal Service post card mailing rate or stamp. The card must be formatted to a specific size to qualify for this rate.

Posters: Large printed items intended for display. Can help shape your brand in the minds of viewers.

Direct Mail: Also called "junk mail," but still a useful means for reaching households and individuals via their postal mail box. A bulk mail account and a minimum number of pieces is required to qualify for the rate. Non-profit organizations also qualify for the lowest possible mailing rates. Bulk mail must be pre-sorted by zip code and properly bundled for mailing. This usually requires hiring a mailing service to properly prep bulk mail.

Print Ads: Advertising in newspapers and magazines.

Radio Ads: Offers the advantage of reaching a target audience depending on the radio station format: R&B, Gospel, Country, etc. Expensive.

Television Ads: Promises to reach the largest and most diverse audiences, but requires many days and weeks of ads to be effective. Very expensive.

Transit Ads: Advertising on public transportation like the bus or subway.

Billboards: The largest ad space.

Door Hangers: A printed item designed with a hook for hanging on door handles. Can only be placed by persons walking door to door.

Production Tools

Script writer: A creative person who knows how to write in a manner that can be filmed or performed.

Video Camera: There are many types of cameras for all levels of quality.

Pro audio gear: Quality and durable equipment such as microphones, mixers, amplifiers, etc.

Page Scanner: Can digitize image and graphics for use with editing software like Adobe Photoshop and for use in print layouts and the web. Some scanners also come with Optical Character Recognition (OCR) software to convert pages to text that can be edited.

Still Camera: From mobile phone cameras, to Point-and-shoot, up to professional level DSLR (Digital Single Lens Reflex) cameras. The type of camera to use depends on the requirements of the project.

Portable audio recorder: It is sometimes necessary to capture audio while away from a production suite or workstation. Many devices will suffice for voice recording including some of the newer smart phones that have good microphones and suitable software. Recording audio using a built-in microphone in a room is not feasible.

Production Workstation: This is a Windows or Macintosh computer dedicated for use in graphic, video or audio production. It is a system with a large amount of RAM, fast multiple processors and one or more large hard drives. This system is optimized for processor intensive projects.

Stock music: It is best, and legal, to use music licensed for productions intended for public presentation. This music can be purchased on CDs or through online sources. Unlicensed music used on videos published to YouTube will likely be removed for copyright violation.

Color Laser Printer: Color laser printers offer high quality printing at a greater value than using inkjet printers. The better printers can print duplex, or two sided.

Audio Editing Software: Original audio often needs "sweetening" or editing to correct levels, remove noise or unwanted dialog.

Video Editing Software: All video requires some type of editing. HD video editing works best on a production workstation. High end software yields the best options and results. Adobe Premier Pro and Apple Final Cut Studio are the common choices among pros.

Page Layout Software: Preparing layouts for flyers, post cards, posters, brochures and all other similar projects require a good software tool with capabilities of correctly handing fonts, import images and provide output options from local printing to pre-press files suitable for offset printing. Adobe InDesign is one of the best tools in this area. Among the worst tools for page layout are MS Word and MS Publisher.

Stock images account: Stock images work like stock music in principle. We want to respect the rights of artists and designs by not simply ripping images from the web. Services like *iStockPhoto.com* offer thousands of quality images for royalty free use in your print or web projects

Image Editing Software: Graphics and photos require preparation for use with print, web, and presentation on screens. One size image does not fit all. Resolutions and file type will vary depending on the output destination. Adobe Photoshop continues to be the tool of choice since the late 1980s.

Presentation Tools

Video Projector: LCD and DLP video projectors continue to provide the best value for projecting large graphics and video. Some of the factors in selecting a projector are the brightness, rated as Lumens and the type of lens used, whether fixed or zoom. For medium-size screens in rooms with normal light, 2,500 to 3,000 lumens should be the adequate. For large rooms with large screens and brighter lighting, 4,000 to 6,000 lumens will be needed.

The cost of projectors rise with the lumens rating and lens type. Newer projectors accept high definition HDMI and VGA-HV inputs, along with the usual analog inputs.

Projection screens: Projection screens can be specialized video screens, or white/off-white walls. Wall or hanging screens are engineered to provided the brightest reflection of light and better rejection of ambient room light. No wall screen can produced true blacks. The absence of light in an image that gives the impression of black. As much unwanted light that can be kept off a screen, the better the contrast.

LCD or Plasma displays LCD displays, including the thinner LED backlit systems offer stunning image quality in rooms of almost any light level. Along with displays using plasma technology, these types of displays have become commonplace. Churches can use specialized devices to deliver content to the displays or run cables to each display from a dedicated computer. Providing a signal to multiple displays over long HD quality cables will require a signal splitter and amplifier to insure crisp images. Be sure to purchase displays with resolutions of 1080p or better. Beware of cheaper screens that are limited to 720p.

PowerPoint or Keynote Software: Microsoft PowerPoint is a capable application for delivering presentation graphics. Apple's Keynote application provides the same function with a superior look and feel. PowerPoint presentations suffer from the overuse of special effects, cheesy clip art and all-too-familiar backgrounds. If you use PowerPoint, try to make it not look like PowerPoint by using custom graphics and fonts other than Times and Arial.

Hanging Banners: Commercial inkjet printers can produce large high quality banners from files created using programs like Photoshop. These type banners are more pleasing than vinyl letter banners, but not as durable.

Freestanding Banners: Floor standing banners are very elegant and useful additions to any display. Better products allow the banner to retract inside the base of the stand like a window shade. These are not inexpensive, but provide great impact.

Spokesperson: Persons who possess a convincing and pleasant voice for projects that require narration.

DVD Authoring Software: Many churches record video direct to DVD recorders. This should be considered a last resort since original video content is compressed to a format that makes editing nearly impossible. Recording to hard drives and importing editing video to programs like Adobe Encore, Apple DVD Studio Pro, or iDVD are the best solutions.

Video Compression Software: Native video, such as HD, is much too large to manage for use with presentations. For uses such as PowerPoint, posting to Facebook or YouTube, it is helpful to compress video before uploading. Good compression yields the smallest file size with a minimum of compression "artifacts" around the edges of images. Uncompressed video produces stuttering playback on average computers, and long upload times. Presently, the H.264 format offers best mix of compression quality with the smallest file size.

 Below is a *Toolbox Assessment* and checklist. After doing some level of strategic thinking and planning for media/new media projects, this checklist can be helpful in selecting tools and tactics needed to get the job done.

Some of your needed resources may come from outside your ministry through products and services offered by freelance personnel, companies or consultants. Depending on the project and budget, tools and personnel may be scaled up or down.

New Media Toolbox Assessment & Checklist:

Item:	Our Present Status:
Personnel Tools:	**Availability:**
Coordinator/Producer	[ ] Staff [ ] Volunteer [ ] No [ ] Outsourced
Art Director	[ ] In-House Staff [ ] In-House Volunteer [ ] Don't Have
Graphic Designer	[ ] In-House Staff [ ] In-House Volunteer [ ] Don't Have
Digital Video producer	[ ] In-House Staff [ ] In-House Volunteer [ ] Don't Have
Web Designer	[ ] In-House Staff [ ] In-House Volunteer [ ] Don't Have
Outside Consultant	[ ] Have Access [ ] Don't Have
Production Assistant	[ ] In-House Staff [ ] In-House Volunteer [ ] Don't Have
Writer/Proofreader	[ ] In-House Staff [ ] In-House Volunteer [ ] Don't Have
Other_____	

Promotional Tools:	**Have used in past or currently using:**
E-mail Blast Capability	[ ] Yes [ ] No [ ] What is this?
Website (up to date)	[ ] Yes [ ] No [ ] What is this?
Flyers	[ ] Yes [ ] No [ ] What is this?
Digital Sign (LCD/Plasma)	[ ] Yes [ ] No [ ] What is this?
Press Release	[ ] Yes [ ] No [ ] What is this?
Social Networks	[ ] Yes [ ] No [ ] What is this? Which ones:_____
Print Newsletter	[ ] Yes [ ] No [ ] What is this?
Senior Leader Blog	[ ] Yes [ ] No [ ] What is this?
Webcast / On Demand Video	[ ] Yes [ ] No [ ] What is this?
CDs/DVDs (Produced in house)	[ ] Yes [ ] No [ ] What is this?
Banner Ads (Internet)	[ ] Yes [ ] No [ ] What is this?
Google Ads	[ ] Yes [ ] No [ ] What is this?
Video Greeting	[ ] Yes [ ] No [ ] What is this?
Brochures	[ ] Yes [ ] No [ ] What is this?
Post Cards	[ ] Yes [ ] No [ ] What is this?
Posters	[ ] Yes [ ] No [ ] What is this?
Direct Mail	[ ] Yes [ ] No [ ] What is this?
Print Ads	[ ] Yes [ ] No [ ] What is this?
Radio Ads	[ ] Yes [ ] No [ ] What is this?
Television Ads	[ ] Yes [ ] No [ ] What is this?
Transit Ads	[ ] Yes [ ] No [ ] What is this?
Billboards	[ ] Yes [ ] No [ ] What is this?
Door Hangers	[ ] Yes [ ] No [ ] What is this?
Other_____	

New Media Toolbox Assessment & Checklist:

Item: **Our Present Status:**

Production Tools

Script writer	[ ] Yes [ ] No [ ] What is this?
Video Camera	[ ] Yes [ ] No [ ] What is this?
Pro audio gear	[ ] Yes [ ] No [ ] What is this?
Page Scanner	[ ] Yes [ ] No [ ] What is this?
Still Camera (High Quality)	[ ] Yes [ ] No [ ] What is this?
Portable audio recording	[ ] Yes [ ] No [ ] What is this?
Production Computer	[ ] Yes [ ] No [ ] What is this?
Stock music	[ ] Yes [ ] No [ ] What is this?
Color Laser Printer	[ ] Yes [ ] No [ ] What is this?
Audio Editing Software	[ ] Yes [ ] No [ ] What is this?
Video Editing Software	[ ] Yes [ ] No [ ] What is this?
Page Layout Software	[ ] Yes [ ] No [ ] What is this?
Stock images account	[ ] Yes [ ] No [ ] What is this?
Image Editing Software	[ ] Yes [ ] No [ ] What is this?

Other_____

Presentation Tools

Video Projector	[ ] Yes [ ] No [ ] What is this?
Projection screens	[ ] Yes [ ] No [ ] What is this?
LCD or plasma screen in foyer	[ ] Yes [ ] No [ ] What is this?
PowerPoint/Keynote Software	[ ] Yes [ ] No [ ] What is this?
Hanging Banners	[ ] Yes [ ] No [ ] What is this?
Freestanding Banners	[ ] Yes [ ] No [ ] What is this?
Floor or tabletop Displays	[ ] Yes [ ] No [ ] What is this?
Spokesperson	[ ] Yes [ ] No [ ] What is this?
DVD Authoring Software	[ ] Yes [ ] No [ ] What is this?
Portable audio/video rig	[ ] Yes [ ] No [ ] What is this?

Other_____

CHAPTER FIFTEEN
What Makes a Good Website?

I have never met a pastor or senior leader who did not want a website for his church. At the same time, many leaders have been disappointed by companies and individuals who promised to develop a website for the ministry who either did not follow through or created a site that was not very usable.

There are six primary ways to develop a website:

Templates:

If the website needs are simple, templates can be a nice solution. Website maintenance is the main challenge. All site updates must be done by a volunteer or a ministry staff member. Templates offer limited flexibility in adding special features or customizing the design.

Volunteers and staff persons with greater responsibilities in the ministry may have difficulty keeping the template website current. Many template websites are published unfinished with pages lacking content showing messages such as, "Add photo here."

Over time, the monthly costs associated with a template website will approach the one time cost of a custom website, but lack the polish, usability and refinement of a custom solution.

Content Management Systems (CMS):

Content Management Systems begin with a template design, yet offer more powerful features than simple template-based websites. CMS uses modules for items such as calendars, integrated blogs, and photo galleries. All updates are made using a web browser, which makes updates more convenient for individuals who may share in web maintenance. Two popular CMS solutions are *Drupal.com* and *Mambo.com.*

Volunteers:

Someone in the church who is an enthusiast or has taken a class may volunteer to create a website for the ministry. The pastor may find it difficult to critique the work out of concern for seeming to be ungrateful. Web development is very time-consuming and therefore difficult for a volunteer to do only on evenings and weekends. While volunteers may be enthusiastic about helping the church, that enthusiasm usually fades over the course of time as the work becomes tedious or demanding. For these reasons, I do not recommend that you allow volunteers to develop your website. On the other hand, it is a good idea to allow volunteers to update professionally developed website content, such as calendars, or other zones within the website designed for that purpose.

Brokers:

Some ministries hire a broker who works for another company that does web development services. I recommend caution when working with brokers for web development. The motivation for many brokers is to sign up as many clients as possible. Most are not experts who are devoted to the craft of web development. Sometimes brokers are connected to companies that operate a multi-level marketing scheme where the emphasis is placed more on the volume of sales than on providing expertise and useful solutions. Ultimately, you end up paying hundreds of dollars for a web package, making monthly payments, having very little direct support, and doing most of the work yourself.

Blogs:

A Web Log or "blog" offers the most affordable solution for website development. A blog is a kind of template website that is formatted for periodic entries. A blog is an online journal or diary. More than all the other types of websites, blogs need more "care and feeding" since entries are normally date and time stamped. If a blog is not updated, the whole world knows it.

While blogs have been used mainly by individuals, the new breed of blogs can be used by organizations. The one key feature that makes blogs usable as websites is something called "static pages." A static page is always available when users visit. It includes navigation links such as "Home" and "Contact Us." Pure blogs push old posts down as new posts are created. An organization website needs some elements and links to be familiar to regular users. Google's free blog solution, *Blogger*, added the option of static pages in June of 2010. This was a feature already available to premier blogging platforms like *WordPress*, *TypePad* and *SquareSpace*. As with template and CMS websites, a staff person or volunteer must take responsibility for setting up the blog and keeping content fresh.

Custom Web Development:

If high quality and having a sustainable web presence is the goal, custom web development offers the greatest value. Value addresses the question: *How much will we receive for the money invested?* Custom web development is priced according to requested features. Unlike other types of development, custom development does not burden the client with the responsibility to populate and maintain their own website. The custom development option can offer greater value for the following reasons:

1. Consultation about strategic considerations for the ministry.

2. Better integration of current and future ministry priorities and services from a tactical perspective.

3. Unique design and style.

4. Customization of features such as e-commerce or e-learning.

5. Outsourcing of maintenance responsibilities.

6. Better variety among pages.

7. Better integration of ministry content.

8. Access to experts for updates, changes and special needs.

9. Greater capabilities for using media such as images, documents, audio, and video

The old saying is true: *"Beauty is in the eye of the beholder."* One person can seemingly hate a car that another person loves. A room color can please the wife while completely displeasing the husband. Everyone has an inherent sense of acceptable or unacceptable style. People may be hard wired in this manner but can be persuaded to accept an unfamiliar style if it is considered useful.

Usefulness or usability is the first objective of good design. Appearance is easy to change. Poor functionality is more difficult to change. A website can have a pleasing appearance, but if it is difficult to use, the initial positive reaction to its appearance will soon be lost. Make good usability the first priority of your website.

Usability Checklist:

1. **Don't make users think too much:** The technical term for this is "cognitive load." If people have to figure out what to do when visiting your website, they'll simply move on. The options on each page should be limited and clear so that users can simply click.

   . *Try This: Count the number of options or actionable items on a web page. Think about how those items are useful given the purpose of the web page.*

2. **Don't waste users' time:** This may be one of the greatest downsides of using Flash on a web page. Flash designers and website owners think a fancy animation is the greatest thing since sliced bread. It is impressive, but quickly loses appeal for frequent visitors. Respect the time and

patience of your users. Help them get straight to the information they want from your website. High resolution graphics or photos are another drag on users' patience. These items must be optimized for fast download or left off a web page.

Try This: Set up a group of people who can test your website while you observe. Notice their actions with the mouse.

3. **Manage to focus users' attention:** Once you are clear about the primary purpose of a given web page or website, be sure to focus the attention of users on items you would like them to interact with. Key statements and words set in larger fonts get noticed. A well designed graphic or concise video clip also gets noticed. The placement of these items determines how they are noticed. In western culture, we tend to read from upper left to lower right. Therefore, items placed high and to the left or center-left get noticed first. The eye also tends to scan from larger to smaller objects.

4. **Pay attention to "the fold."** This is the point at which items cannot be seen on the screen without scrolling down. Newspaper designers know that everything below the fold cannot be seen when a folded newspaper is laying in the newsstand or on the table. Good web design also follows this principle. Too often, designers work on their huge computer displays and forget that the average person will view content on smaller displays. The rapid increase of mobile devices such as the iPhone or iPad creates an additional challenge for designing for good usability.

5. **Use accurate, effective words:** Do not allow poor wording on your website. Misspellings or overly worded sections only attract negative attention. Initial visits to web pages are more a visual and emotional experience than a cognitive experience. Concise statements are essential to keeping users engaged. If they are interested, they will find and read the sections that contain more substantive information. Websites don't have to be "dumbed down."

There are users who enjoy reading insightful, thorough writing, but this content cannot be placed at the "entrance." Again, people tend to scan websites on the way to heavier content if they want it.

6. **Keep it simple:** Websites like *CNN.com* or *NYTimes.com* are complex by design. The complexity is presented in a highly organized manner, but this would never work for a ministry website. *The church is the only organization in the world that does not primarily exist for the benefit of its members.* We exist for the benefit of others. This fact requires simplicity of design and ease of use. *Simplicity does not mean simplistic. A simplistic* approach seeks to make light of serious concerns. *Simplicity* makes it easier to handle complex and serious matters.

   Simplicity in design seeks to move people from simple to complex. For example, a home page may have a simple, usable appearance with a fewer, well placed items. The home page hides complexity and makes it available as needed by users in "chunks" or by related groups of items. People who want to post a prayer request don't need to see the 10 part Bible study on the Names of God.

7. **Don't be afraid of the white space:** "White space" is another term borrowed from print design. A good magazine design separates elements with white space. Text and images are not crowded together. They are allowed to breathe and allow the readers to feel more at ease. While the white space in web design may not be white in color, the idea is to create a sense of ease and openness in the minds of the users by making good use of spacing.

8. **Use the TETO principle:** *"Test Early, Test Often"* is the mantra of good web design. All web browsers behave differently. The World Wide Web is based on standards. However, the reality is that Microsoft, Apple, Mozilla, Google and others all have their own twist on how we should view content on the Internet. Add to this mix the emergence of mobile computing, designers have to test on every kind of computer, web browser and mobile de-

vice. If your web pages do not load on all devices (out-dated computers/web browsers excepted), you are not fulfilling the digital equivalent of the Great Commission to *"Go into all the world...."*

9. **Refresh and Update:** Plan on refreshing or updating home page content on a weekly or monthly basis. Reward visitors to your website by offering fresh images, messages or streaming content. Keeping the website up to date is one of the most important features in making your website "sticky." *Stickiness* is a buzzword for websites that users want to visit regularly. There is no definitive, sure-fire list of preferred elements since websites differ in purpose and target audience. For a ministry website, items such as lively daily devotionals, instant polls, or weekly sermon media could provide some stickiness. The response to new elements introduced to a website can be measured using tools that measure website traffic. All web hosting companies offer utilities that provide metrics on website usage. Google offers a service called *Analytics* that can be enabled to measure traffic to your website.

10. **Go easy with** *"Eye Candy."* We have all been to websites that initially dazzled us with lots of movement, animation, and things blinking and flashing. This might be appropriate for an amusement park website or an entertainment website that is competing for the limited attention of visitors. A website that you expect to be frequently visited by your partners and friends, should not be annoying or slow loading because of excessive graphics or flash animations. When I come to a website with a dramatic flash animation I look for the *"Skip This"* button. Eye candy such as flash animations are easy to sell to clients who have not thought deeply about the importance of usability.

11. **Design with Mobile in Mind:** Design decisions introduce certain trade offs. For example, iPhone and iPad web browsers do not support Flash. For a while, design-

ers were content to ignore iPhones and use Flash anyway. Now, since tens of millions of people use iPhones
and similar devices, forcing the use of Flash limits the
reach of your websites.

 *(Some content retrieved from: www.smashingmagazine.com – 10-
principles-of-effective-web-design}*

CHAPTER SIXTEEN
So You Want to Do Video?

Digital video happens at many levels. Many devices have video recording capability, from cell phones, to MP3 players, to digital cameras, to compact HD camcorders, to "Prosumer" (Professional/consumer hybrids), and all the way up to $100,000 digital film rigs.

The wide variety of choices has brought considerable confusion into the arena. The present wave of digital video follows the same pattern as the Desktop Publishing revolution of the late 1980s. The Macintosh suddenly put graphic design hardware and software in the hands of anyone who could afford to buy a Mac. Windows soon followed with applications such as Publisher.

What was once a field owned by professionals and dedicated enthusiasts, saw "graphic designers" spring up everywhere. The same has occurred today with digital video. Since the barrier to entry has been lowered, many have come on board producing content we could describe as, *"the good, the bad, and the ugly."* Some professionals consider the influx of untrained enthusiasts as a threat to their business. There may be some truth to this assertion. Enthusiasts, who have day jobs, are willing to accept projects paying little to nothing—undercutting persons who make a living in the field working at or near market rates.

On the other hand, the separation between excellence and mediocrity will always exist. There are always potential clients who recognize excellence and choose to pay for it, though they also expect high value for their investment.

On balance, this commoditization of digital video is a good thing. It is good because the tools for digital video creation are available to anyone who wants to discover them. Talented young people have easier access to professional level tools for exploration and learning.

Since 2000, I have conducted summer Media Camps for urban youth in Indianapolis and workshops at various times during the year. These programs include exploration and learning in new media areas such as digital video production, web development, photography, graphic design, interactive media and more. Youth ages 11-18 use the same professional gear and workstations that we use in our new media company. Some of our young people have gone on to pursue careers in media. Others have gained skills that they can use in almost any field of endeavor. This would not have been possible without affordable hardware and software.

Video Production Process

Video production generally unfolds in three phases followed by final output:

- **Pre-Production:** Pre-production is the most important, and least expensive, phase since it involves thinking, looking at project specifications, and working through decisions on paper. Anything overlooked in pre-production can cause production and post-production to take longer and cost more. Fixing problems and making changes is more difficult during the later stages. Problems can include actions not properly rehearsed, props not obtained, incomplete scripts, wrong footage captured, and much more.

- **Production:** The creation of the production assets such as filming talent, creating graphics, animation, video effects, audio products including voice overs, music, and sound effects.

- **Post-Production:** Video Editing, titles, other needed effects, and final cuts for review.

- **Project Delivery Format:** DVD, Broadcast tape, Blu-Ray, web delivery or presentation to screens in High or Standard Definition.

Some Types of Video Production

Spontaneous: Unplanned video captured using any available device. Intended to capture a memory or humor family and friends.

Community: Planned and unplanned video captured and edited to share among communities of individuals such as clubs, classes, groups of Christians or other persons who have a shared interest.

Public Service: Brief and powerful messages designed to inform and persuade the public on a particular topic.

Journalistic: Intended as an objective report of an event. Follows general principles for journalistic integrity.

Corporate: A polished video intended to inform, train, or persuade stakeholders.

Illustration Videos: These are videos in the form of short films written to illustrate a subject or sermon. *Sermon-Spice.com* specializes in this genre.

Commercial: Video production commissioned by individuals or organizations to meet specific business or organizational objectives. Projects may include promotional content, television programs, webcasts, live event recording, music videos and more.

Documentary: Telling the story about someone or something. Normally requires substantial planning, gathering information, script writing and many hours filming and editing. Second only to film in complexity.

Film: Many movies today are filmed using specialized digital film cameras such as Arri, Red or Panavision. These devices have resolutions *four times higher* than High Definition and better.

A Few Guidelines for Shooting Better Video with Consumer Cameras

Large ministries have the means to invest in professional-level video equipment and hire expert personnel. Small to medium size ministries often go with consumer and prosumer equipment. It is possible to achieve very good quality with non-professional gear if the limitations of the equipment are respected and if persons have a commitment to learn and follow professional-level principles.

1. **Make the commitment to include as much quality as your equipment and skills will allow**. Because video has become accessible on a number of devices, the ease of creating video can lead to a kind of laziness with technique. Unlike musical performances or audio recording, people seem to be content with recording and exhibiting bad video. In fact, we are currently experiencing an *epidemic* of bad video coming from churches. Organizations that would not approve of singing out of tune or selling CDs with distorted audio, seem to be content with permitting bad video. Once a low standard becomes acceptable by persons not committed to excellence, the low standard becomes the norm. More importantly, poorly executed products like bad video does not help the witness of the church to the world we want to reach for Christ.

2. **Know your equipment.** For video, the *automatic* setting is mainly useful in ideal situations. If automatic is the only option, work within its limitations.

3. **Get good gear.** Ministries and serious video enthusiasts should invest in a camcorder with the following minimum features: HD format (720p, 1080i, or 1080p), manual white balance, manual exposure, external audio input, headphone jack, image stabilization, removable record-

ing media, tripod thread on bottom.

4. **Audio is as important as the video.** If the camera cannot accept external audio, avoid filming an event with a presenter on the stage and the loudspeakers far away. *Tip: Setup closer to the loudspeaker for better on-camera sound, even if you cannot maintain a center view.*

5. **Fill the frame.** Make sure your subject is not a small object in the video frame. Get closer or zoom in.

6. **Use a tripod,** monopod, railing or something stable as a shooting platform. Shaky video is unwatchable! *Only your mother and friends will enjoy watching your shaky video!* Cameras with image stabilization also benefit from a steady hand.

7. **Avoid much zooming** while in the shot: Stop filming, zoom to re-frame, and continue filming.

 Digital video tutorials and techniques available at www.newmediaforministry.com/book

Webcasts & Streaming media

Streaming media has become mainstream as websites such as YouTube stream millions of video clips to millions of users every day. Websites such as *CNN.com* and other news organizations regularly post video clips of news stories, and other current events. Today, many churches embed YouTube video they have uploaded to their websites.

Posting videos online is straightforward: Content from a camcorder is captured to a computer, edited as needed, compressed, and then uploaded directly to a video sharing website. YouTube and other services like Vimeo are capable of HD quality. Achieving this quality requires an HD workflow during filming, editing, and final compression for upload. Low quality video cannot be greatly improved, so always capture at the highest setting.

Using free video sharing websites is a good idea if you want to share your messages and content with a diverse audience.

It is also good to consider solutions for streaming media that do not rely on free services like YouTube. The advantage to this method is that you can control access to your content. Also, there are no limitations on content length. Providing on-demand streaming video from your ministry requires a web hosting account and knowledge of how to compress, upload and deploy video.

If you require customized services for video, you can go with services such as *StreamingMinistry.tv* (operated by the author) and *BrightCove.com*. These companies will take your video content and do the conversion for you.

Are you ready to go live?

With the many benefits of increased Internet bandwidth has come the opportunity to share live events via the Internet. Both audio and video can be delivered in real time using relatively simple tools. There are both professional and free web-based resources for delivering live content. On the professional side, there are solutions like *TriCaster* (www.newtek.com/tricaster) and *WireCast* (www.telestream.net) that will convert a Windows or Macintosh computer into a live production switcher. This application can receive input from both audio sources and camcorders, allowing you to add titles and special effects, then webcasts the resulting signal using a built-in streaming server or through a service like Ustream.com.

Free web-based applications include services such as *Ustream.com*, *Justin.TV*, and *LiveStream.com* that accept signals from audio and video sources via Firewire and USB. These signals are transferred to the host server and then redistributed over the Internet. Many of these services also allow recording and storage of the live stream for later on-demand viewing.

Live web streaming or webcasting requires a fast upload speed from your computer. Many Internet providers boast about their fast download speeds, but offer meager upload speeds. A good quality webcast requires a *minimum* upload speed of 512 kbps. Check your Internet speed using services like SpeakEasy Speed Test (*speakeasy.net/speedtest*). You will also need to limit other Internet activity on your network when webcasting. Your Internet connection is like a water pipe with limited pressure: The more people turn on faucets, the less water becomes available to all faucets.

Live streaming can be unpredictable. There is a saying that goes: *"Murphy lives in the live feed."* You probably have already heard about something called "Murphy's Law." It goes like this, "If anything can go wrong it will go wrong." There are a host of challenges and problems that go with delivering a live video stream. Delivering live audio, however, is relatively easy in comparison to delivering live video.

Those who have met with disappointments and disasters in trying to deliver live content over the Internet have come to a general conclusion: It is better to *time shift* content rather than attempting to deliver that content live. Time shifting is the practice of recording content, compressing it, and making it available on-demand. Content can be time shifted by as little as an hour or two. The benefits of time shifting include:

1. Content can be recorded at a higher quality than available during a live webcast.

2. Content may be edited to removed unwanted sections before making it available on-demand.

3. Titles and graphics can be added, including an opening or closing sequence.

 More about video setups, webcasting and on-demand at the companion website.

Closing Thoughts

New Media for Ministry has covered a number of relevant topics. As stated in the introduction, this is not an exhaustive guide. There is more information available about many of the topics covered in this book. The companion website, *www.newmediaforministry.com/book* will continue to be updated with helpful and current information about new media as it relates to ministry.

Readers are also invited to share their knowledge and insights while visiting the website. Your input will not only inform fellow leaders and laborers in Christ, but provide ideas for future editions of *New Media for Ministry*.

Below are two excellent books that I recommend. These resources offer additional insight on the role of media to the work of God.   ~ *Rev. Bryan Hudson*

Recommended Reading

Wired Church 2.0
Len Wilson with Jason Moore. ISBN: 978-0687648993
Visit *www.thewiredchurch2.com*

The New Media Frontier
John Mark Reynolds and Roger Overton. ISBN: 978-1433502118
Visit *www.crossway.org*

Contact the Author

Bryan Hudson
4625 North Keystone Avenue
Indianapolis, Indiana 46205
(317) 758-7404

Visit Online

twitter.com/BryanHudson | **Twitter**
BryanHudson.com | **Blog**
newcovenant.org | **Ministry**
visionmultimedia.org | **Youth Media Empowerment**
visioncomsolutions.com | **Consulting & Production Services**

New Media Glossary

 Help improve this glossary by suggesting new additions and corrections at the companion website.

Atom Feed - An XML file that encodes web content - usually from blogs. A user can subscribe to an Atom feed and read updated content from a newsreader, web site or handheld device. The process is known as syndication and companies are increasingly using this approach to communicate with employees, partners and customers.

AIFF (Audio Interchange File Format) - The audio format native to Macintosh computers.

Anti-aliasing - The blurring of hard edges to create the appearance of smoothness. Most commonly used with respect to graphics, especially text.

Aspect Ratio - The ratio of the width of a film frame to its height. Now often 1.85 to 1, in the "studio era" it was 4 to 3 (the 1.33:1 "Academy ratio" still used for TV). Wider ratios like Panavision (2.2:1) and Cinemascope (2.55:1) are closer to what our eyes actually see, but need increasingly anamorphic lenses for photography and projection, and are difficult to translate to television. The more contemporary HDTV format has an aspect ratio 16:9.

Audio - The term "audio" is synonymous with sound and is used more in TV production than in motion picture production; as in "audio/video" ("sound-and-picture").

AVI (Audio Video Interleaved) - A Microsoft format for digital audio and video playback from Windows 3.1. Somewhat cross-platform, but mostly a Windows format. Has been replaced by the ASF format, but still used by some multimedia developers.

Bandwidth - A measure of the amount of data that can travel through a network. Usually measured in kilobits per second (Kbps). For example, a modem line often has a bandwidth of 56.6 Kbps, and an Ethernet line has a bandwidth of 10 Mbps (10 million bits per second).

Bit Rate - The number of bits transmitted per second. In theory, a 56 Kbps modem, for example, can transmit up to 56,000 bits per second.

Boom Microphone - A pole-like device used to project the microphone over a set, and out of camera range, to pick up the sound of dialogue. It can be quickly lengthened or shortened according to need, and pointed in any direction as required.

Blog - Blog is an abbreviated version of Weblog, which is a term used to describe Web sites that maintain an ongoing chronicle of information. A blog is a frequently updated, personal Web site featuring diary-type commentary and links to articles or other Web sites. Blogs range from the personal to the political and can focus on one narrow subject or a whole range of subjects.

Blog Aggregator - A web site that keeps track of blog posts. There is usually a search box and RSS updates. Submitting a blog to an aggregator can increase exposure and get your content in front of a wider audience.

Blogosphere - A common term used to describe the large and diverse community of people who contribute to blogs. Some bloggers are very influential and reach a large audience, allowing news to travel quickly among this community. This is the factor causing many companies to monitor and reach out to the blogosphere to protect and promote their brand identity.

Bookmark - A browser function that allows users to store links to specific web pages at their fingertips. This makes it easier to return to favorite web pages. Web sites, such as delicious, allow users to organize their bookmarks, share them with others, and access them from other computers.

Browser - A World Wide Web client. An information retrieval tool.

Buffering - A process used as a part of streaming media technologies whereby a certain amount of data is fed into the player (such as the RealPlayer) to allow it to begin playing before fully downloading the file.

Byte - One of the basic units for measuring digital information, especially relevant to understanding storage capacity on computer disks. 8 bits comprise a byte. Roughly 1000 bytes equals one kilobyte. 1000 kilobytes is one megabyte or MB. 1000 megabytes is a gigabyte.

Cache - Has a number of specialized meanings, but the most common refers to the computer memory that stores information that is most frequently used. Usually stored in a special section of the main memory or in a separate device, this data can be retrieved much faster than if the computer has to find it on the hard drive.

Client - The software that allows users the ability to retrieve information from the Internet and World Wide Web. Netscape is an example of client software.

Close-Captioned (CC) - A system which displays the current dialog on screen for deaf or hard-of-hearing viewers. Contrast with subtitles.

Cloud

CMYK (Cyan, Magenta, Yellow, and Black) - A color model used when working with print-based images that describes colors as mixtures of cyan, magenta, yellow, and black ink. CMYK is contrasted to the RGB (Red, Green, Blue) color model, which is used when working with images intended for electronic presentation, such as on computer monitors, televisions, and LCD screens.

CODEC (Coder/Decoder) - A mathematical system for compressing (encoding) and decompressing (playing back) a video or audio file. CODECs can be hardware or software-based, or both. Hardware CODECS are often more efficient, but the trade-off is that not all users will have the special hardware needed to play back the file.

Color Correction - In imaging, this refers to the process of matching the colors in a digital reproduction of an image to an analog original, such as a photograph. Adobe Photoshop is the standard application for color-correcting images. In film, this refers to adjusting the final print so that colors match from shot to shot, regardless of the film stock and camera used.

Compression - The process of reducing the size of a media file by eliminating data. Higher compression means that the compression utility (usually a software program or a combination of hardware and software) defines greater amounts of data (such as larger areas of an image) as redundant, but at certain points the human eye will register the missing information as quality loss. The trade-off is that highly compressed images can be delivered more efficiently over a network.

Creative Commons - A nonprofit organization that promotes free public licenses to content (creativecommons.org/). Creative Commons provides specific conditions through which content can be reused, such as attributions, links or other notification methods to correctly identify the original source.

For companies that want to maintain ownership of content – but also want to spread the content – Creative Commons Licensing is an effective approach.

Data Rate - An attribute assigned to a media file by a compression utility. It is a measure of the amount of digital information transmitted in a given unit of time — usually a second. Thus, a video could be encoded to play back at a rate of 500 kbps. The data rate set for a file is usually influenced by the limitations of the target delivery medium. CDs, for instance, generally have a maximum transfer rate of 300 kbps.

Decoder - A piece of hardware or software that is used to convert video or audio (typically) from the digital form used in transmission or storage into a form that can be viewed.

Digital Audio - Audio that has been encoded in a digital form for processing, storage, or transmission

Digital Editing - Editing a portion of a movie by digitizing one or more frames and altering them electronically or combining them with other digitized images, and then printing the modified frame.

Digitize - To convert analog (wave-based) media into digital format (zeros and ones) so that they can be understood by computers. Also known as "capturing," and sometimes "encoding." Digitization of video is usually accomplished with add-on devices for computers known as "Video Capture Cards," although firewire ports, which are increasingly becoming a standard on out-of-the-box systems for both Mac's and PCs, can perform this function. Audio can normally be digitized through standard sound cards that come with most computers.

Download - To move a digital file (such as a media file) from a server where it is stored to a local system for viewing or editing.

DLP Projector - A type of video projector capable of high brightness and contrast.

DPI (Dots Per Inch) - A measure of printer resolution.

DRM (Digital Rights Management) - A technology that allows content owners to determine and control who and how users can view content such as media files on the Internet.

Dubbing - The technique of combining multiple sound components into one. Can also refer to automatic dialog replacement of another language.

DVD (Digital Video Disk or Digital Versatile Disk) - An emerging medium for storing large amounts of digital data, most notably movies encoded using MPEG-2 compression (a CODEC designed especially for use with DVDs). DVDs can hold several gigabytes on a single disc. Most CDs by contrast can only hold 600 megabytes each.

DVD-ROM - A drive capable of reading DVD disks. DVD-ROM drives are usually backward-compatible, which means that they are also capable of reading CD-ROMs and audio CDs.

DVD-Video - A standard that combines DVD disks, MPEG-2 video compression, and any of a number of high-quality audio formats to create a movie that is stored and played back on computers and on DVD players designed for home entertainment centers.

Editing - The selecting and joining together of shots in the way they will appear on the movie screen. The work progresses from assembly to rough cut, then fine cut, at which point the sound editor is usually brought in.

Editing, Non-linear - *see Non-linear Editing*

Embed Tag - An HTML tag used to place a media file (such as an audio, video, or Flash file) into a web page. The embed tag defines an area on the page in which the media file will appear if it involves graphic elements, helps the browser understand what type of file it is, and specifies other information as well, such as whether the file will play automatically when the page loads. Embedded media are contrasted to media controlled through a separate player, such as when the RealPlayer pops up over your web browser to display a video.

Encoding - The process of compressing a media file for a specific purpose, such as streaming on the Web, One can encode a file that is in analog form (such as a VHS tape) or one that is already digital (such as the signal on a Mini-DV tape).

Feed - The most common type of web content syndication. Feeds are generally done via RSS or ATOM (see definitions). By subscribing to a feed, a user can consume content from blogs, wikis, websites, or other frequently updated content through their "feed reader" without having to constantly visit the content source online. Depending on the type of reader a user chooses, RSS and ATOM feeds can be consumed in a browser, via e-mail, or on a mobile device.

Firewall - A security measure that prohibits users in certain local area networks (LANs), such as one belonging to a corporation, from receiving or sending certain types of digital content. Some firewalls prevent the transmission of audio and video files.

Flash - An animation and video delivery platform. Popular on desktop computers but losing favor with mobile devices

Frame - In the world of film and photography, this refers to one of the many individual images that comprise a roll of exposed film. In the digital world it refers to one of the many discrete still images that comprise a digital video or animation file.

Frames Per Second (fps) - The number of video frames displayed each second (also called frame rate). Most people perceive continuous motion at about 17 fps. A common standard for video delivered over the web is 15 fps, which reduces file sizes substantially (since most video is shot at roughly 30 fps) but still but allows for fairly smooth motion.

FTP (File Transfer Protocol) - The process of moving files back and forth between a server and a local computer.

Gigabyte (GB) - A unit of measure equal to 1,000 megabytes.

H.264 - A high quality, scalable video CODEC used for video delivery from web resolutions up to Blu-Ray and HD brodcasting.

HDTV – High Definition Television.

HTML (HyperText Markup Language) - The rules that govern the way we create documents so that can be read by a WWW Browser. Most documents that are displayed by Mosaic are HTML documents. These documents are characterized by the .html or .htm file extension . For example: homepage.html or homepage.htm

HTTP (HyperText Transport Protocol) - The protocol through which web pages are transmitted over the Internet.

HTML5 - An emerging web content delivery platform in 2010. May replace technologies like Flash especially on mobile devices

Hyperlink - A link in a given document to information within another document. These links are usually represented by highlighted words or images. The user also has the option to underline these hyperlinks.

Interlaced - Images that are displayed progressively as they download. Interlaced images appear to come into focus gradually in contrast to images that are not interlaced, which are drawn from top down as they download.

Internet - The international computer network of networks that connect government, academic and business institutions.

IP (Internet Protocol) - The basic language of the Internet. It was developed by the government for use in connecting multiple computer networks.

ISP (Internet Service Provider) - A company that allows users to dial in to the Internet usually through a modem. Other services ISPs often support include web hosting, the ability for users to maintain their own websites, and e-mail.

Java - An object-oriented programming language that is platform independent (i.e., works on Windows, Mac OS, Linux). Java is often used to write "java applets," which are small applications that can be embedded into web pages, giving the pages sophisticated functionality.

JavaScript - A programming language based on Java and C++ developed by Netscape that allows web authors to give increased interactive functionality to web pages. Common functions created with JavaScript are image rollovers (an image that changes when you scroll your mouse over it), browser detection, and pop-up windows.

JPEG (Joint Photographic Experts Group) - Refers to an image file format popular for delivery over the Web because of its relatively high quality and low file size. Before uploading JPEGs to the Web, users can determine the amount of compression assigned to them-usually on a scale from 1 to 10. Recommended file type for photographic images.

Kilobyte - A unit of measure equal to 1,000 bytes.

Letterboxing - A technique marked by black strips at the top and bottom of a screen image that allows for video or film shot at wide aspect ratios to be viewed on devices such as standard televisions that have squarer shapes.

Long Tail - A writer for Wired Magazine, Chris Anderson, has applied this statistical concept to web businesses (the long-tail represents the outer parts of a bell-curve). For example, a brick-and-mortar retailer could not justify stocking products that have minimal demand (at the long-tail). However, retailers like Amazon.com can essentially have unlimited shelf-space and thus benefit from long-tail market opportunities.

Megabyte (MB) - A unit of measure equal to 1,000 kilobytes.

Metadata - Data included with a website, digital photo or other embeded digital resources

MPEG (Moving Picture Experts Group) - A series of International Organization for Standardization (ISO) standards for digital video and audio, designed for different uses and data rates.

MPEG-2 - The standard for DVD video. Supports higher data rates than MPEG-1.

Multicast - In streaming media, it is the method of carrying a compressed video signal across multiple routers to various clients.

Non-linear Editing - The computer-assisted editing of video without the need to assemble it in linear sequence. The video-editing equivalent of word processing.

NTSC - The video input signal formats used in North America and Japan. Full-sized NTSC has a display rate of 60 fields per second (30 interlaced fps), and 525 total lines (480 visible) per frame.

PAL (Phase Alternating Line) - The European standard for television transmission.

Pan and Scan (aka Full Screen) - A process by which significant action in film is determined on a shot-by-shot basis, and less significant parts are eliminated to fit onto a television-sized screen. A way of compensating for television's narrow aspect ratio when transferring film to video. Contrast with Letterboxing.

PDF (Portable Document Format) - A proprietary document format from Adobe that preserves formatting such as specific fonts and graphics by embedding them into the file. PDF files are created with Adobe Acrobat.

Pixel - A single unit of screen information: one of the colored "dots" that make up a video image. Depending on the display mode, a pixel may require 8 bits/1 byte of information (for 256, or VGA, color mode), 16 bits/2 bytes (for "high color" mode) or 24 bits/3 bytes (for "true color" mode).

PNG (Portable Network Graphics) - An image file format designed for the Web. Supported by Microsoft Internet Explorer 4 and Navigator Navigator 4.04 and later.

Podcast - A podcast is a media file that is distributed over the Internet using syndication feeds, for playback on portable media players and personal computers. The host or author of a podcast is often called a podcaster. Though podcasters' Web sites may also offer direct download or streaming of their content, a podcast is distinguished from other digital audio formats by its ability to be downloaded automatically, using software capable of reading feed formats such as RSS or Atom.

Peer to peer (P2P) - Just as the Network Effect is creating unparalleled access to a global customer base, the Internet's availability of computing power & resources is also creating the new business models. Peer to Peer (P2P) applications rely primarily on the computing power and bandwidth of the participants in the network vs. having to provision large centralized data centers. This P2P architecture enables new services to be launched with much less capital expenditure and operational resources.

QuickTime - A digital audio and video file-format and architecture developed by Apple Computer, Inc.. Can be viewed on most computing platforms.

RSS (Really Simple Syndication) - A form of syndication that lets users "subscribe" to receive new or updated content from blogs, news, or other frequently updated online content sources. RSS is a simple format which can be easily implemented by website administrators and easily consumed by it's consumers. RSS feeds are typically received by a "newsreader" inside a user's browser or e-mail program - some applications can also send RSS feeds to mobile devices.

Increasingly, corporations are using RSS as a way to communicate with customers and prospects by making RSS an option for newsletters, product updates and other messages. Inside the enterprise, RSS is becoming a common way to help employees overcome "information overload."

Search Engine Optimization (SEO) - SEO is an important component of an overall Web marketing strategy. It is the process of improving the quantity and quality of traffic to a website from search engines. Typically, the earlier a site is presented in the search results, or the higher it "ranks," the more users will select the corresponding links.

Social Networking - This is using the web to communicate with friends, colleagues and even strangers. Social-networking sites have been in existence since the early days of the Internet. Many of the sites involve personal activities, such as dating. However, some corporations – like LinkedIn (www.linkedin.com) have leveraged social-networks for business purposes.

Streaming Media - Video or audio transmitted over a network that users can begin to play immediately instead of waiting for the entire file to download. Typically a few seconds of data is sent ahead and buffered in case of network transmission delays. (Although some data is buffered to the hard drive, it is written to temporary storage and is gone once viewing is complete.) RealMedia, QuickTime and Windows Media are the most common streaming formats.

Surround Sound - A sound system which creates the illusion of multi-directional sound through speaker placement and signal processing. See also Dolby, SDDS, DTS, THX.

Tag - A tag is a (relevant) keyword or term associated with a piece of information (like a picture, article, Web site, or video clip), thus describing the item. Typically, an item will have more than one tag associated with it. Tags are chosen informally and personally by the author/creator or the consumer of the item - i.e. not as part of some formally defined classification scheme.

TCP/IP - Transmission Control Protocol/Internet Protocol, a set of rules that establish the method with which data is transmitted over the Internet between two computers. **Teleconferencing -** *see Videoconferencing*

Terabyte (TB) - A unit of measure equal to 1,000 gigabytes.

TIFF (Tagged Image File Format) - An image file output format. TIFF files are lossless, meaning the compression they apply to an image doesn't create artifacts that can degrade the appearance of the image. TIFF files are often used for archiving high quality versions of an images, such as images intended to be reproduced in print or studied digitally in minute detail.

URL - Uniform Resource Locator, the address to a source of information. The URL contains four distinct parts, the protocol type, the machine name, the directory path and the file name. For example: *media.ucsc.edu*

VOIP - Voice Over IP (Interent Protocol) is the popular name for a standard or "protocol" that allows the Internet to be used as a telephone.

Video Conferencing - Two or more people who are geographically distant having a meeting across a telecommunications link such as IP, ISDN, or T-1 line. Sometimes called teleconferencing.

Web 2.0 - See Chapter Four, *"What is Web 2.0"*

Web browser - *see Browser*

Webcast - Webcasting is sending audio and/or video live over the Internet. In essence, Webcasting can be thought of as broadcasting over the Internet. A Webcast uses streaming media technology to distribute non-streaming media like radio and television over telecommunications networks, to take a single content source and distribute it to many simultaneous listeners/viewers. The ability to Webcast using cheap/accessible technology has allowed independent media to flourish.

White Balance - A way of calibrating a camera's color response to take into account different color temperatures of light (i.e., fluorescent light is greenish; sunlight, more blue; incandescent light, yellowish). This calibration allows the camera to define what the color white is under any of these various lighting conditions. Failure to white balance could result in an unsightly, unnatural color cast. Better camcorders have automatic and manual white balancing controls.

Wiki - A wiki is a Web site that allows visitors to add, remove, edit and change content. It also allows for linking among any number of pages. This ease of interaction and operation makes a wiki an effective tool for mass collaborative authoring. The term wiki also can refer to the collaborative software itself (wiki engine) that facilitates the operation of such a site, or to certain specific wiki sites, like encyclopedias such as Wikipedia.

Widescreen (aka Letterbox) - Technically, a particularly wide aspect ratio used for some films, but commonly used to describe content (such as appears on many DVDs) that displays at wider aspect ratios than are normally in use, such as on standard televisions.

Windows Media - A media format developed by Microsoft for streaming and playing back media files.

XML (eXtensible Markup Language) - An standard for describing, or marking up, documents and data distributed on the Web. XML allows authors to create customized tags that can help them efficiently achieve their goals.

Notes

Notes

Notes